KRP

W9-DHN-646

YOU ARE MY BELOVED!

YOU ARE MY BELOVED!

Sermons
for
Ash Wednesday to Pentecost

Frederick W. Kemper
and
George M. Bass

Publishing House
St. Louis

Unless otherwise indicated the Scripture quotations in this publication are from the Revised Standard Version of the Bible, copyrighted 1946, 1952, © 1971, 1973 by the Division of Christian Education of the National Council of the Churches of Christ in the U.S.A., and used by permission.

Concordia Publishing House, St. Louis, Missouri
Copyright © 1981 Concordia Publishing House

MANUFACTURED IN THE UNITED STATES OF AMERICA

1   2   3   4   5   6   7   8   9   10   WP   89   88   87   86   85   84   83   82   81   80

Library of Congress Cataloging in Publication Data

Kemper, Frederick W.
    You are my beloved.

        1. Church year sermons.   2. Lutheran Church—
Sermons.   3. Sermons, American.   I. Bass,
George M joint author.   II. Title.
BX8066.K38Y68   252′.62   80-19734
ISBN 0-570-03821-9

Contents

Foreword

The church year observed by Christians since earliest times did not fall together accidentally. Even a superficial look at its structure reveals a logical purpose and development behind the various seasons and cycles.

The Lenten season, as it is known and observed in the liturgical churches, has undergone considerable expansion, as well as some distortion. The Sundays in Lent, for instance, were not considered a part of Lent. The Passion of our Lord was originally observed during Holy Week, culminating in the Easter Vigil and the dawning of Easter.

Easter, however, over the centuries has become "the living end" of a solemn observance of Lent, even extending backward to pre-Lent, whereas it was meant to be the center of the Christian's faith and liturgy, moving and motivating the Baptism-reborn believer toward Pentecost.

The popular observance of Lent has been conditioned by many forces—as has been the lost observance of the Easter Vigil. Gone is much of the morose piety that marked the Lents of our childhood. The church is more and more concerned about a proper observance of Lent and Easter. It can do no better than to return to and reclaim the principles and rationale behind the centuries-old structure of the Paschal season, as it was so clearly laid out in the old standard lectionary.

Note—as the earliest fathers did—the central place of Baptism. Read the old lessons, introits, and collects for Easter and the Sundays after Easter. "The newborn babes" who are to desire the sincere milk of the Word are the newly baptized believers who can never forget the experience of Easter Eve, and each recurring observance of that event with its 12 readings from the Old Testament was a reminder and reinforcement of their instruction in the faith and their new birth in Baptism.

It is this centrality of Baptism that the church is trying to restore to the liturgy by making the Easter Vigil the fulcrum of the Lent to Pentecost path the child of God takes. Luther thought so highly of this now casually treated event and doctrine that he preached 23 sermons on Baptism. Yet this initiatory sacrament, commanded in the Great Commission, gets scant mention even in Lutheran preaching throughout the church year. This Lent to Pentecost series of sermons is meant to correct that imbalance by comparing the "baptisms" of Jesus—His water baptism in the Jordan and the "baptism" of His crucifixion with their meaning for our adoption as God's children.

The theme for this *You Are My Beloved* series has a two-fold thrust: The midweek series *(You Are My Beloved Son)* directs this affirmation of God to His only begotten Son, Jesus Christ. He said this to His Son and about His Son vocally on two occasions: at His baptism and at His transfiguration, and visually, for all the world to witness, as He hung on the cross in ultimate obedience to His Father's will.

The Sunday sermons from Lent I to Pentecost use as their theme the implied affirmation of the same God-Father to His children in Baptism, when He says in effect, "You Are My Beloved Children!"

The texts for this series are selected from the list of readings set for the Easter Vigil, reviewing the process by which God's eternal plan was carried out to make a special people and family for Himself. The texts from Easter to Pentecost consider the drastic effects of Baptism in the Christian.

The pre-Easter emphasis is catechetical in nature, affording a rich opportunity for Lutherans (and others) to review the elements of their faith. The post-Easter texts look at the results and effects of the baptismal covenant and relationship and lead to a natural transition of the believer from disciple to apostle, from follower to witness: all derived from the contemplation and acceptance of Christ's "baptisms" for us.

The use of all the Sunday morning texts provides an opportunity for a richer and more meaningful observance of Lent—though one may end the series at Easter. In either case, the emphasis is Biblical, Baptismal, and liturgically authentic and can only lead—we hope and pray—to a greater appreciation of that miracle by which we find ourselves children of God and can call Him "Father."

The Publisher

YOU ARE MY BELOVED SON

**Sermons
for
Midweek Lenten Services**

by Frederick W. Kemper

Ash Wednesday

The Plan

Scripture Readings: Mark 15:33-39; John 1:1-4, 14;
Luke 1:26-35; Luke 2:10-14

Text: Mark 15:39

Precisely nine months before the zero hour that marks the beginning of the Christian era, Jehovah God revealed His unique Personhood in a humble home in Nazareth. Throughout the Old Testament times the people of the covenant knew a great many things about God. They knew Him as Creator and Preserver of our little planet Earth and the whole galaxy system of which our earth is such an infinitely small corner. They knew Him as a gentle God whose outstanding attribute was "steadfast love," but at the same time they knew Him as a God of rigid justice. They knew that at many strategic moments God had intervened in history. They knew that God had a plan to rescue them from the predicament in which mankind found himself, brought upon the whole human race by the sin of Adam at the very onset of history. If they knew the God who is three distinct Persons in one divine Essence, they did not fully comprehend it until the angel Gabriel visited a peasant girl named Mary in her home at Nazareth.

Discovery of the Blessed Trinity

There, in a moment fraught with more significance than the birth of our Lord Jesus Christ at the stable, behind an inn in Bethlehem, the plan of God for rescuing man from God's own sentence against man's sin was advanced with the Self-disclosure of such proportion and of such deep mystery that man, wiser for the knowledge yet incapable of comprehending it, must make the "leap of faith" to accept it all.

The solution to man's predicament was resolved in the councils of the Godhead before the world began. The problem arose by the pronouncement of man's eternal damnation for his disobedience in the Garden of Eden. Man had betrayed the intolerable compliment of freedom of the will with which God had entrusted him. The terms of the

11

covenant that forbade man to eat of the tree of good and evil had been breached. "In the day that thou eatest thereof thou shalt surely die" (Gen. 2:17 KJV). Justice demanded of a faithful God that the conditions of the covenant be met. Failing that, justice demanded that the penalty it demanded be carried out. Yet such was the love of God for His creature, man, that the council of the Godhead set the plan in motion to resolve the awesome dilemma posed by the tragedy of Eden. It was the decision of the council that one of the Godhead persons should submit Himself in man's stead to the unspeakable justice of God. Thus by coming in love for the unlovely, sinful world, by submitting to the Law and the punishment for transgressing it, and through suffering the awesome wrath of God harbored against the sinner—by substituting Himself He could sustain the justice and demonstrate the love which God had for His beloved creature. In Him both justice and love would be served.

Nine months before the precise beginning of the Christian era, God revealed His Trinitarian essence to the world. An angel broke the barrier of invisibility and stood before the virgin Mary. His message was both brief and awesome. "Do not be afraid, Mary, God has been gracious to you; you shall conceive and bear a Son. You shall call His name Jesus. He will be called the Son of the Most High." Mary expressed her perplexity. "I am a virgin," she said. "How can these things be?" To which the angel answered, "The Holy Spirit will come upon you, and the power of the Most High shall overshadow you. Therefore the Child will be called the Son of God." Mary accepted the mystery, the responsibility, the consequences, the will of her God.

Few moments in the annals of history carry more revelation than this one in a humble dwelling in Nazareth. It is precisely at this place and at this time that the Son, that Person of the Trinity who had agreed in the councils to come to our earth for our redemption, is revealed as the Son.

The whole idea of the Trinity remains the supreme mystery of God. The Christian church wrestled with the problem of "three Persons yet one God." That is, for us, in itself a contradiction. The church came at last to leave the mystery a mystery and make the leap of faith and accept, as Christians must always do, the record of Scripture. The Athanasian Creed is the church's supreme statement of the relation of the three Persons to each other: "Among these three persons none is before or after another, none is greater or less than another, but all three persons are coequal and coeternal."

The Plan

But the implications of the Nazareth event do not end with the disclosure of the Trinity. It sets into motion the divine plan for the reconciliation of the world to God. To understand the plan at all one has to start with the problem. The problem is sin, not simply mine or yours, but ours together. John the Baptist would one day point at Jesus and cry, "Behold, the Lamb of God who takes away the sin of the world!" (John 1:29). Sin here is the great mass of sin. It is the sum total, the staggering total of all the sins of all mankind. As many people as there are in the world, each with his own mass of daily sins—of his mind and mouth and hands—and his own life's total of sins and all these masses heaped together in a total super-mass, these are the "sin" of the world. In the judgment of God any one sin is deadly, damning. Multiply the sin by millions and multiply it again and again. The extent is staggering; the sum total of the all is beyond imagination.

To think of the number of sins you have to remember the sin of Adam (whom God forgave in view of the plan). You have to think of Amorites and Hittites, of the Greeks and the Romans, the Seleucids and the Turks. You have to remember the lame man on a stretcher, blind Bartimaeus, and the Centurion's son, Lazarus, and the thieves on the crosses with Jesus. You have to think of contemporary demographic tables that say there are over 4½ billion people living in this year of our Lord 1981, and you have to remember that all of us "daily sin much and indeed deserve nothing but punishment."

The plan, long expected by the prophets and the faithful, hopeful people of pre-Christian times, was put into effect at Nazareth. That Person of the blessed Trinity, the Son, elected to the task, entered human existence at its absolute beginning. Mystery of mysteries, God in human flesh subsisting. Mystery of mysteries, the majesty, the power, the glory of God in embryo subsisting. No wonder the angels broke the midnight skies to announce His birth, or that angel choruses sang a glory song at His first appearing. No wonder Mary pondered these things in her heart.

It is appropriate that the Father name His Son. With the plan in mind instructions were given to the angel messenger. "She is to call My Child Jesus," the Father said, and in the name the Child's destiny was sealed, for Jesus means Deliverer. Because He would face the problem of sin and judgment, that the world might be saved, He was called Jesus. Joseph was given similar instruction by the angel that appeared to him, "You shall call His name Jesus." On the eighth day after His birth, when Mary and Joseph took Him to the temple to be circumcised after the practice of the Jews, they called Him Jesus, even as the angel had instructed them.

The Plan Is Set in Motion

In the fullness of time, that is in God's appointed time, the plan began to unfold. When Jesus was baptized by John, the Father,

13

speaking from the clouds, claimed Him as His Son: "You are My beloved Son; with You I am well pleased" (Mark 1:11). "My beloved Son!" In our finiteness we are forced to think of God in human terms to understand Him even a trace. "You are My beloved Son." How personal, how warm, the Father is as He addresses His Son. The Father's heart is showing; the Father's love is showing. The Father is reaffirming His Fatherhood and affirming the Sonship of Jesus in glowing terms of human relationships. "You, Jesus, are indeed My Son, even as Your mother has told You. Like a human father, I love You." Even as He spoke, the Father looked down the long road His Son would walk and saw—hell, for the plan moved in this precise moment into its second phase. Before long the Father would abandon His Son to hell. The plan demanded it. Reconciliation depended on it.

Nor is Jesus free from the terrible implications of this moment. On the one hand the silence of God since the strange mysteries that surrounded His birth has been broken. Now all His mother's stories have been vindicated. "Has not God spoken to Me? Has He not called Me Son? If then I am His Son, I shall be a Son." He knew the meaning of the father-son relationship. It opened to Him the Father's heart, and it set Him on the road to hell. The plan had been devised; the plan must be carried out. Such was the intention of God at the announcement of His conception. Now, at His baptism, the intention moves into new motion.

A comparison suggests itself. A dam is built above a city to impound water. For many years the dam has stood strong and dependable. One terrible day, when rains filled the reservoir to capacity, the dam gave way. The whole city, lying in the path of the terrible rushing waters, was destroyed. Nothing but an act of God could have saved it. Just so the wrath of God against the sin of the world reached impossible proportions. Soon the love that had stayed judgment so long must give way to His justice. By an act of God humanity is spared His judgment. The plan interposed the very Son of God between the judgment against sin and humanity. The Son would take into His own body the sins, and the judgment against them—against us all. God's judgment against sin must be held inviolate. God's love for the world, for people, must not be denied. The plan had been devised so that justice might have its due and that love in the end might be triumphant.

In due course Jesus sets His face toward Jerusalem. He would stand ready to meet our fate head-on. He would interpose Himself, in love for all of us sinners, between us and judgment, between us and the terrible wrath of the Father. He faced His accusers in the backrooms of ex-high priest Annas, and He heard the terrible sentence of high priest Caiaphas in the temple meeting rooms. He stayed silent before the cruel mockery of King Herod, and accepted the king's betrayal without flinching. He

14

stood before Pilate; He heard Himself pronounced innocent; He watched with dismay as Pilate washed His hands, and thus gave signal that Jesus was as good as dead already as far as he was concerned. Down, down, down! Down into the darkness on Calvary. Down into the abyss of hell. Down into our damnation. Down into our hell. Down beneath the teeming wrath of God. No wonder the Father hid His face. No wonder Satan danced at His death. No wonder contemplation of the cross of Jesus brings tears. No wonder Christians through the ages, contemplating the awesomeness of Calvary, have wept—and marked themselves with ashes as the season of the meditation on the passion of the Son of God began.

Resolution of the Plan

In that awesome hour Jesus redeemed the world, redeemed us. "Weeping may," as the Psalmist says, "endure for a night, but joy cometh in the morning" (Ps. 30:5 KJV). Jesus, for the "joy that was set before Him, endured the cross" for us! The tragedy is a triumph; death brings life; despair has become hope, because the Father, through His only-begotten, His beloved Son, is reconciled again to the world. "Glory to God in the highest, and on earth peace and good will to men."

The last word on Calvary came from a Roman soldier. He was a centurion charged with carrying out the death sentence on Jesus. He spoke more to himself than for anyone standing near, but he summed up the events of a day and of a lifetime in the ultimate statement that everyone who would find peace with an angry God must say. He surely didn't know about the angel's visit to a virgin girl in Nazareth. If he had heard about it at all, he probably would have dismissed the Christmas story out of hand. It is questionable if he attended the gathering where 5,000 ate bread and fish, or if he put any stock in the rumor that Lazarus had been raised from the dead. He had only the events at the Crucifixion to go on. The Victim had prayed for the Father to forgive those who had judged and crucified Him. He had endured the taunts and mockery of the chief priests and the soldiers and the citizenry with infinite patience. He had prayed that the Father might take His spirit. The centurion heard the last breath escape from Jesus at the end when He could no longer force Himself up to the beam to gasp air. He knew the signs of death when he saw them, "Truly," he said, simply and profoundly, "this was the Son of God."

The Father, if one may speak of Him in human terms, may have turned to the mighty angels who stood nearby. "This," He could have said, "this is My beloved Son in whom I am well pleased." And we, to whom the Spirit has given faith, can but echo Him, "Jesus is the Son of God, My Savior and my Friend." Amen.

15

Response

Scripture Readings: Matthew 3:13—4:11; Exodus 14:19-31;
   1 Corinthians 10:1-4

Text: Matthew 3:13—4:11

John's baptism in the Jordan waters was not something new under the sun . . . at least not as far as baptism itself was concerned. One form of Jewish baptism authenticated second-generation Israelites. The fathers had passed through the Red Sea experience, which in the minds of succeeding generations made them true sons and daughters of Israel. A baptism was instituted in which the experience could be symbolically duplicated and a person thus authenticated as a true Israelite. Again, Gentiles were baptized long before John appeared on the scene. In this baptism the converts foreswore all that they had been outside the Israelitish faith, including their families, were cleansed of these Gentile marks in the baptismal waters, and entered into the life and faith of the Jews.

John came preaching a baptism of repentance for the remission of sin in anticipation of the coming of the kingdom of God. He brought to the concept of baptism a whole new dimension. He preached the Law, for he was the last of the Old Testament prophets; he announced the imminence of Christ and His kingdom, for he was the forerunner of the Messiah. People came to the river to hear him preach. "What must we do?" they asked; and John, speaking from the Law, instructed them in righteous living. Always the theme of his message was "repent." Repentance presupposes alienation from God, sinfulness, a need to change direction. In full knowledge of their sinfulness, the people answered John's call and stepped into the water to receive his baptism.

When God's hour was right, Jesus came to John to receive John's baptism. Jesus, the Son of the living God, was without sin; He had done nothing in all His years to alienate God. Surely He did not need John's baptism of forgiveness. As He walked into the water, He was doing a most exceptional act, for He was identifying Himself with sinners. The

16

sinless One, the Son of God, through His deliberate act, publicly identifed Himself with all sinful humanity. From this moment on He was radically involved in the sin, the burden, the damnation of the whole human family. The judgment of God must now fall on Him in the name of all sinners; His guiltlessness must stay that judgment and turn it into forgiveness for humanity with which He had identified Himself.

The stage play *The Deputy* was written by Rolf Hochhuth after World War II as an indictment of the church for its silence during the holocaust in Germany, one of the most evil events in contemporary history. Riccardo, the protagonist, has discovered the awful truth of the extermination camps for the Jews. He seeks to make the truth known. He finds no ear. At last he identifies himself with the Jews and moves to his death with them, for it is beyond him how else to protest. Wearing a yellow star he arrives at the concentration camp. The horrors of it almost overwhelm him. He is ultimately condemned to the gas chambers and dies an unsung martyr, true to his convictions to the end.

John understood his baptism to be for sinners. He protested Jesus' baptism, when Jesus asked to receive it. At the very least, if Jesus is to be baptized by John in the sinner's baptism, it can mean nothing less than that He is taking His place with sinners. He stands with them in the water; He identifies Himself with them. The world, unwittingly, has been placed on notice. This is the Messiah, the promised One, the saving One, promised by God through the prophets of old, who has come to seek and to save those who were lost.

The voice from heaven should not surprise us, now. As He stepped out of the baptismal waters (Luke says He paused to pray), the voice of the Father was heard from the heavens. "This is My beloved Son, with whom I am well pleased." The words, the voice, the message confirm the initiation of the second phase of the divine plan by which the world should be redeemed. Out of obscurity into public life, out of filial devotion to His mother into full-fledged devotion to His Father—and to the plan for the salvation of the world.

The Holy Spirit, in the form of a dove, was there, too. For the second time (the first having been at the Annunciation) the Godhead of the Trinity was "visible." Matthew in the King James Version, introduces each appearance with a much-deserved "lo!" "Lo! a voice," and again, "Lo! . . . the Spirit of God descending!" We must add our own lo! to Matthew's. Lo! the Son of God—who has identified Himself with sinners.

The Temptation Experience

From His baptism Jesus went immediately to the wilderness retreat. He must spend time in meditation. He must wrestle with the fact of His Sonship. "What does it mean for My life that I am the Son of God? If that is who I am, what then is My purpose and My destiny?"

Matthew informs us He fasted. The masters of the spiritual life tell us what the spontaneous self-denying fast is like. First it is simply a matter of hunger, which vanishes in a few days. Without nourishment the body lives on its stored up food. Once this is gone, the body begins to attack the vital organs. Hunger now becomes intense and life is threatened. But the process frees the spirit. The sense of reality lessens. At length the defenses we build around ourselves fall away. The soul is bared. There is danger now of confusion, of a kind of giddiness of the spirit. It is at this point of the fast that Satan came into the wilderness.

His attack, as well one might expect, is at the very point of Jesus' meditation. "If You are the Son of God . . . isn't it time to prove it to Yourself? Son of God, indeed! Exercise Your power, do miracles, if You are the Son of God. Test Your Father's love for You by casting Yourself from this pinnacle. I can offer You a shortcut to glory; just bend Your knee a trifle and the glory is all Yours."

But in the process of fasting and meditation, Jesus had reached His conclusion. "I am the Son of God, therefore, wonder of wonders, I have God for Father with all the closeness, all the oneness that implies. I can commune with Him in prayers, for His heart is open to Me. I have His love and protection. He will watch over and comfort Me.

"And I will act in obedience to My Father's will. I will do nothing, think nothing, say nothing that is not in the Father's purposes for Me. Yes, Father. Yes!" In the wilderness Jesus said yes to the Father and in His yes His life took on meaning and purpose. Once He had spoken His yes, once life had a purpose, He could not live anything but yes. It didn't matter now where life would take Him, what it would demand of Him. He was committed to the Father and to the Father's will for Him. He had identified Himself with sinners at John's baptism; if the sinner must suffer the judgment of God, so let judgment come. He had submitted Himself to the Father's will. Nothing could be taken from Him, for in perfect obedience nothing belonged to Him. The plan for the redemption of the world had carefully been laid out. He said yes to His awesome part of it.

Paul Gerhardt, the Lutheran poet and hymn writer of the 17th century, caught the spirit of all this in his Lenten hymn entitled "A Lamb Goes Uncomplaining Forth." The Father turns to the Son and speaks,

> "Go forth, My Son" (the Father saith),
> "And free men from the fear of death,
> From guilt and condemnation."

to which the Son replies,

"Yea, Father, yea, most willingly
I'll bear what Thou commandest;
My will conforms to Thy decree,
I do what Thou demandest."

Satan's attempt to seduce Jesus failed. His rebuttal to Satan's choices grew out of His faithful yes. "Man does not live by bread alone, but by the word of God." His yes denied Him bread, freed His spirit, and rebuked Satan. "You shall worship the Lord, your God, and Him only shall you serve." His yes to God denied Him escape from the plan, which had as its end the cross. The seduction attempt of Satan was futile; the testing of the Father was past. Angels, the account says, came and ministered to Him.

Illustrations of the Principle

Dag Hammarskjöld, who was to become Secretary General of the United Nations, relates in his book *Markings* (a kind of diary of thoughts that intrigued him, whether his own or others) how he had inherited a belief that life only became meaningful and acceptable through selfless service to his country or to humanity from his father's side of the family. From his mother's side the idea was ingrained that all men are equals as children of God and are so to be treated. He read the accounts of medieval mystics, who after the example of Jesus had learned to say yes to every situation where their neighbors had need, and to whatever situation life might demand of them. The mystics lived by love in its highest senses. In their self-surrender they accepted without reservation whatever life demanded of them of work to be done, suffering to be endured, or happiness to be enjoyed.

As he matured, these three forces converged in his thinking. On Pentecost 1961 his entry in his diary refers to the moment when he said yes to God. It was at that moment that his life became meaningful and had a goal in self-surrender. He appreciated anew the life of Jesus who had said yes to God so long before. He knew then that Jesus' yes was in every line of the gospels, in the garden when He must drink the cup of suffering, in the cross when He prayed for His enemies and commended His spirit to the Father. So Dag Hammarskjöld, having said his yes, didn't look back any longer, nor did he worry about the future. He was under the dominion of God.

Literature has many heros of self-surrender, of high commitment. A case in point is T. S. Eliot's drama *Murder in the Cathedral*, in which the Archbishop of Canterbury, Thomas à Becket, faced martyrdom at the hands of King Henry II. He had refused to sign the Constitution of Clarendon, which denied the Church of England freedom from civil jurisdiction. In his Christmas sermon, an interlude in the plot, Eliot has

19

Becket say that martyrdom is never the decision of man. True martyrs are instruments of God who have lost their will in His and no longer desire anything for themselves. Soon Becket was stabbed to death in his cathedral for what he was convinced was the will of God which he must uphold at any cost.

And Our Response

The process through which our yes to God comes differs with each of us. We were baptized, most of us, as little children. Through our baptism, like Moses who was brought into the palace of the pharaoh, we were brought into the household of God. We were singled out and branded with the guarantee of the Holy Spirit. Our parents, in most cases, brought us to Sunday school and worried us through church. If we were lucky we attended a parochial school. Somewhere, somehow the processes at work, with the power of the Spirit ever present in them, pressured us (or are pressuring us) to say yes to God. The decision must be made in each generation, for we cannot trade on another's faith. The decision must be made alone, for none of us can make this decision for another. Prayer before God must happen, with searching and straining. Then at last, all praise to the Holy Spirit, it came, it comes. The load of what we are by nature and who we are by birth and what we have become in life fall off as we bow our heads before the Father and say our yes. We have truly entered the "eye of the needle" and begun life in the family of which God is Father and in which Jesus is Brother.

To be called a son or daughter of God presupposes that we have said our yes to God. Our yes, in response to God's great self-disclosure to us and response to His mighty promises to us, presupposes that we have accepted the wonder of communion with God. It means we have access to the Father's house and heart. We are in daily conversation with Him in our prayers. We enjoy the warmth and security of His great God heart. It is special; it is exciting; it is sheer joy to know God as Father and to be part and parcel of the Father's family.

But yes to God carries with it the responsibility of obedience to Him. Our yes means we seek out the will of God for us. We are under His dominion. We are as sons and daughters at His disposal free to serve Him. We search His will out of the Holy Scripture, and if the injunction is to "love your neighbor—and your enemy," so be it, for the love of the Father we will love him.

It means we have broken with the past, for we are no longer self-seeking, no longer serving other masters. It means leaving the future to God's direction. If He leads into tragedy or triumph, it is He who leads. Courage is replaced with faith; the goal is immediate; we will serve God and Him alone. We would emulate Jesus, who in the bitter agony of crucifixion prayed for His persecutors, clung to God in the frightening, lonely darkness in the hour of our hell, who when it was finished, commended His faithful spirit to His faithful Father and died.

Yes to be faithful to God requires that we be faithful in all things and in all events. To fail God by lack of trust, to fail Him by a deliberate decision contrary to the spirit of the Kingdom, is to fail Him utterly. To confess God and then fail Him in trial is mere flight and disgrace. How often that happens . . . with truth, half-truth and lie; with hate and love, with covetousness and contentment, with the choice of whom we shall serve. How often we betray our confession, our yes!

Because of Christ, who said yes to the Father at His baptism, and who maintained His yes in the wilderness through to His life's end on the cross, the Father has endless patience and constant forgiveness for His stumbling, bungling children. He asks only that having stumbled they rise again in His forgiveness and justification to try again to be faithful to Him. That is the glory and the wonder of Christ's victory over sin, and death, and the devil. The Father God, like a human father, patiently— infinitely more patiently than a human father—picks us up when we falter and fall, accepts our sorrow for failing Him, wipes our repentant tears, and as it were, sets us on our feet to try again.

Quietly, or if it be your nature, with whooping and hollering, thank God for His unspeakable gift to us. Christ came. Christ said yes to the Father. Christ fulfilled His mission, obedient to the end. The Father accepted Christ's sacrifice. We can be, we have been, accepted into the family of God, whose patience and love, forgiveness and purpose, joy and peace are the rule by the very example of the Father, wherein life gets purpose and dignity, and above all, a goal for time and for eternity. Amen.

Commitment

Scripture Readings: Mark 10:35-45; Matthew 21:33-46;
   Philippians 1:21-26; Romans 8:31-39

Text: Mark 10:38 (Matthew 20:22-23); Luke 12:50

Captain John, USN, was committed to God, his country, and his family.
Such was his commitment that he would have gone to his death for any
one of them. In the service of his country he commanded submarines in
enemy waters. In the service of his family he was exemplary. In
devotion to God he was unswerving. He died of a heart attack, but those
who knew him remembered him with respect for his sterling example of
loyalty.

Everybody is committed to something. Their commitment shapes
their lives. One person is committed to sports, another to the bottle,
another to his job, still another to God. In the commitment life finds its
meaning and purpose. Even apparent lack of commitment—think of
derelicts and tramps—is a commitment by which life is oriented and
ultimately given form.

Toyohiko Kagawa was a Christian missionary. He was born in
Kobe, Japan, July 10, 1888. He grew up in an upper class, non-Christian
home until his father died. He graduated from high school, whereupon
he announced he planned to study for the Christian ministry. The uncle
with whom he lived promptly disowned him. During his senior year at
the seminary he visited and began work in the Shinkawa slums. Homes
there were six feet square, with five or six people living in each one. Ten
thousand people lived in a ten-block area in terrible filth. Gamblers,
thieves, murderers, prostitutes, and beggars abounded. Tuberculosis,
syphilis, and trachoma were almost universal. In the Christmas season
1908 Kagawa rented a room and moved into the slums. He ministered to
everyone he could and preached the saving Gospel to anyone who
would listen. Time and again he was beaten by thugs who saw him
distributing help out of his $1.50 monthly salary. He was a man of
exceptional talents as his literary, theological, and poetical works show;

but his conviction that he could best serve Christ in the Shinkawa slums never wavered. Toward the end of his life he wrote that "as Christ emptied Himself and became a servant bearing the cross of humanity, I have endeavored to follow Him. Because I have tried to follow in the steps of the Redeemer, I preach a Gospel of redemption." (Toyohiko Kagawa, *The Religion of Jesus*, trans. H. Topping and J. F. Gressit, Philadelphia: John C. Winston Company, 1931.)

Jesus and Commitment

Jesus was committed to our redemption. At His baptism by John the Baptizer, He identified Himself with sinners, for He, as the sinless One, needed no such baptism. In the Jordan waters He set His course toward the cross, where for the sin and the sinners of the world He would endure the awful judgment of the Father against sin and the sinner. So closely involved in His baptism with the cross that they cannot be separated.

Somewhere in the course of His ministry, the sons of Zebedee, James and John, came to Jesus and asked that they be given choice seats when He came into His kingdom. "Ye know not what ye ask," He told them, then went on to ask them, "Can ye drink of the cup that I drink of? and be baptized with the baptism that I am baptized with?" (Mark 10:38 KJV). The Kingdom would not just happen. It could come only through suffering and death. Another time, in the midst of a long discourse with His disciples and followers, He injected the same thought. It is almost as if the thought of the cross never really receded into His subconscious. "But I have a baptism to be baptized with, and how I am constrained until it is accomplished" (Luke 12:50).

Through the whole active ministry of Jesus, our Lord, *His* baptism, the one at the Jordan and the one at Calvary, shaped His life. He was committed to a course and would not deviate from it, no matter what happened along the way. He met with His disciples on the mountain of transfiguration, where He was transfigured before them. Moses and Elijah stepped out of heaven (as it were) and spoke with Him. Notice, He is not permitted in heaven; that is denied Him. The Lawgivers step out of heaven, and they speak of His decease at Jerusalem! Our inclination, like Peter's, is to be overwhelmed by the transfiguration. Jesus, and Moses, and Elijah! Three tents are indeed called for. The event has to be seen from the point of view of Christ. He was kept out of heaven!

The place is Caesarea Philippi. Peter has blurted out his affirmation in response to Jesus' question of His identity. "Thou art the Christ, the Son of the living God!" Peter's confession is absolutely right. Jesus had communicated the awesome truth of His deity, and Peter had grasped it. The lesson is not over. Jesus talked to them of "how He must go unto Jerusalem and suffer many things of the elders and the chief priests and scribes and be killed and be raised again the third day" (Matthew 16:21 KJV). Peter was incensed at such an idea. He rushed up to Jesus, took Him by the shoulder, and rebuked Him for even thinking such a thing. "Get behind Me, Satan!" Jesus said, "thou savorest not the things that be of God, but those that be of men." (vv. 22-23). The will of the Father, the plan of redemption, the commitment of Jesus—these things Peter couldn't fathom, not yet. But the Father knew and Jesus knew. Neither man nor devil would deter Jesus. His face was set toward Jerusalem and the cross.

There is a tender scene in the upper room where Jesus met with His disciples to celebrate the Passover. John remembers and records it. For a moment Jesus needed to pray. He lifted His hands and heart to God, His Father, to lay large petitions at His Father's feet. In full knowledge that soon, soon, He would be pinioned to the cross, that He would be entirely involved in the terrifying business of redemption, that He could not take care of those whom God had given Him, he commended them to the safekeeping of the Father. "Now I am no more in the world," He prayed, "but these are in the world, and I come to Thee. Holy Father, keep through Thine own name those whom Thou hast given Me, that they may be one, as We are One" (John 17:11 KJV). So He sets His house in order. He gives His own to the safekeeping of the Father, for He will not take them into hell with Him.

He prayed in the Garden of Gethsemane. "Father, Father, Father." The holy name of the Father punctuated every sentence of His prayer. The disciples wearied and slept, during the hours He wrestled with the immediacy of the awesome ordeal. They slept when the angel came to Him, as Luke says, "to strengthen Him." Don't read by the Gethsemane angel too quickly. The angel came in the middle of His praying, and when the angel had left "He prayed more earnestly,and His sweat was as it were great drops of blood falling down to the ground" (Luke 22:44 KJV). Have you wondered why? It was because the Father didn't come Himself. No word, no sign from the Father. Imagine yourself in agony somewhere in a hospital, calling for your beloved to come and hold your hand. Your beloved does not come, but sends a messenger boy from the nearest telegraph office to comfort you. Such a messenger the Father sent to His Son, and the Son read His message aright. The Father, who had begun to withdraw from His Son on the transfiguration mountain, has retreated again. The Father's answer to the Son's prayer is "No." The angel was sent to give Him that terrifying word. No wonder His sweating was, as it were, drops of blood falling to the ground.

They arrested Him then and took Him to the trial. The trials were terrible miscarriages of justice. Yet how completely they served the plan. Caiaphas, chief priest in those days, engineered His excommunication from the church—from the body of God's chosen people. Caiaphas stood up, tore his garments with mock grief that the innocent Jesus had been found guilty of blasphemy, and must therefore, according to Jewish law, be put to death. The church, His church, didn't want Him. It cast Him out from its midst.

Herod, symbol of the nation that God had nurtured so carefully, tetrarch of Galilee, found Jesus preposterous and refused to take Him seriously. He put a white tunic on Him, symbol of one who aspires to a political office, and sent Him back to Pilate as a joke. His nation didn't want Him. His nation outlawed Him. His nation didn't care.

The blood of his murder was to fall on Pilate. Pilate represents humanity. Pilate allowed His murder, but refused to accept the blame. He washed his hands of Jesus, a clever gesture that said to the chief priests, "You are responsible!" (see Deut. 21:1-9). They understood, indeed, for they assured Pilate, "His blood be on us." Thus humanity, symbolized by Pontius Pilate sought to escape blame, yet is ultimately responsible for banishing Him to the hill and to the cross.

Now the inhuman cross was before Him. But the cross with its attendant indignity and suffering, was not the worst of it. The judgment of God was there on the hill, in the cross and beyond and beneath the cross—a reality so terrifying we can only guess at its horrendous intensity. God the Father, His Father, shut Him out of His heart out there on Calvary and left Him to suffer the damnation of hell alone. Our damnation, our hell. Abandoned by His church, abandoned by His nation, abandoned by the human community, and now, worst of all, abandoned by the Father. Outlawed, abandoned, forsaken, delivered to Satan in our stead. When the all-consuming waves of damnation had engulfed Him; when He had been faithful to the trust, and only then, He cried with a loud voice, and died.

Thus it should have been with all sinners. This was the fate God had decreed for them, that they should perish in the eternity of hell, forever abandoned by God. But the Son of God came. He identified Himself with sinners on the Jordan's bank. His baptism could not, would not, be finished, until He had carried the sin of the world, and the sins of every sinner, into hell. Voluntarily, He lived knowing that there was no escape from the cross. Voluntarily, He accepted the nails driven by the Roman soldiers—and the abandonment of the Father—for our sakes, for us.

No small wonder that He turned to James and John, who wanted easy access to the seats on either side of His throne. The Kingdom did not come that easily. Nor could they, in spite of their protestations, be baptized with His baptism. No small wonder, indeed, that He was constrained until His baptism should be over.

So our Lord fulfilled His commitment. But to whom shall we say He was committed? To the Father, certainly. Was He not the obedient Son, doing willingly what the Father willed? To the world in rebellion against God? Surely to the world, for He had come to seek and to save the lost. You and me, certainly, for we are numbered with mankind, and in our own right have by our sins incurred judgment against ourselves. "God spared not His own Son but delivered Him up for us all." "God was in Christ reconciling the world unto Himself." And we, who by faith accept Christ's substitution in death for us, we are free from the wrath, from judgment, from the fear of the last enemy, death, because Christ was thus committed to us.

Our Commitment to Jesus

Christ stood on the mountain of Ascension and gave His last command to His disciples and to His church. "Go, teach and baptize all nations in the name of the Father and the Son and the Holy Spirit." Christian baptism drew meaning from Christ's baptism. His death and resurrection brought new meaning and new content to Baptism. St. Paul noted that content in Romans (6), "We are buried with Him by baptism into death, that like as Christ was raised up from the dead by the glory of the Father, even so we also should walk in newness of life" (v. 4 KJV). Newness of life! Sons and daughters of God! that is the meaning and purpose of our baptism, made possible only by our Lord and Savior Jesus Christ, who was baptized (the word is His) at Calvary on a cross.

Toyohiko Kagawa caught the enormity of Christ's sacrifice—and committed himself, as His Christ had done, to serving his fellow human beings. The disciples committed themselves to the saving Christ, and went out to conquer the world for Him. To a man, save only John, they were martyred for this deep commitment. God alone knows how many others committed themselves to the reconciling Christ, only to die the martyr's death. Commitment, to suffer all rather than to fall away from Him, is the necessary fruit of our faith.

The Father said it long ago, "You are My beloved Son." Peter, having caught the vision, echoed it at Caesarea Philippi, "You are the Christ, the Son of the living God." A centurion, standing at the foot of the cross when He died, said it, "Truly, this Man was the Son of God." When we said it after them in our own right, from our own conviction, "Jesus Christ, You are the Son of God indeed," we affirmed our commitment to Him to spend our time before the distant trumpets blow for us, in quiet devotion, in meaningful service to humanity for the love and for the sake of Him who was baptized with water and with fire for us. Amen.

Choices

Scripture Readings: Isaiah 53; John 11:47-57 (John 18:1-11);
Deut. 21:1-9

Text: John 11:50

Lazarus is alive and well! The news spread through Bethany like fire in a windstorm. Before the day was out, it had gotten to Jerusalem. Miracles of miracles. The man had been dead four days when the Carpenter from Nazareth stood at the opening of the grave and called to him, "Lazarus, come forth!" Still in his winding sheets, the man emerged from the gloomy recesses of the tomb. He fell on his knees at Jesus' feet, but the Master bid him go into the house and eat. There is no question he was dead. There is no question he is alive and well.

In Jerusalem the news reached the temple area, and soon it was carried to Caiaphas, chief of the priests in those days. The news was not received there with much joy. It was the topic of conversation in every encounter inside and outside the temple compound. St. John sums up the problem of the religious leaders in a single question: They said, "What shall we do?" and he immediately follows it with the seeming catastrophe the miracle portended for them: "This Man doeth many miracles. If we let Him thus alone, all men will believe on Him, and the Romans shall come and take away both our place and our nation" (John 11:48 KJV).

One can hardly understand the working of the minds of those who saw the miracle. John reminds us that some believed. Miracles like Jesus did, especially this marvel-filled one no man could do unless God be with Him—or more precisely, unless He be God. That surely was one of the functions of the miracles . . . to see behind the event Him who did the sign, and in Him, behind Him, the ultimate power through which the miracle was accomplished. Some looked beyond the event and saw God. But others looked beyond the event and saw only trouble for themselves and for their nation. If Jesus were allowed to continue with this kind of thing the covenant people and their nation would disappear, swallowed up by Rome.

Once the news reached the temple, where the high religious authority lay in the priests and the person of the high priest, there were questions that begged for answers. Is this Man of Satan or is He of God? Does He do these things of Himself or are other powers at work in Him? Who is this Man who raises people from the dead? The priests had the Scriptures. The Scriptures should be consulted—especially by the priests. Isaiah long ago had said that the Lord's Annointed could be recognized when One came by whom the blind would receive their sight, the lame walk, the deaf hear, the dead raised up and poor have the Gospel preached to them (Isaiah 61:1). In the synagog at Nazareth Jesus had applied the Isaiah prophecy to Himself. In Him the prophecy had already been amply fulfilled. The blind were made to see again at His touch, the lame walked again at His command, the deaf heard again at His word, the dead were indeed raised up, good news had come to the poor. There should have been no question had the priests gone to their Bible. It was as plain as Jesus knew how to make it. But they didn't go to the Scripture. They rationalized . . . and the best they could do was see their own demise as a people and a nation if Jesus were allowed to go on.

There were these two poles from which to make choice. Either Jesus was Satan or the Annointed One. If He was Satan He must be expunged from their midst, for they could not tolerate the leadership of one whose power came from the Prince of Darkness. If Jesus was present among them as the Annointed One of God, they must, faithful to their places as God's chosen people who waited for the Messiah, surely fall prostrate before Him. They should have sounded the cry that the Messiah had come and that all should follow Him. They did not consult the Scripture. They wallowed in their dilemma.

But Caiaphas came up with a solution. Not knowing or realizing from whence the words had come, he cast the die. He, in his official position as chief priest, made the decision, quoting Scripture: "It is expedient for one Man to die for the people," he said. Caiaphas, you know not what you are saying! This was the very essence of the plan of the Father already in the Garden of Eden: "I will put enmity between you and the woman, between your seed and her Seed." The plan for the redemption of the world was indeed that One should die for the people! It was in Isaiah again, "All we like sheep have gone astray . . . and the Lord hath laid on Him the iniquity of us all" (Is. 53:6 KJV). That was the plan from the beginning, that One should die for all. Jesus had come for precisely that purpose. In the very language of God, Caiaphas prophecies. In the very presence of God he makes his choice. Jesus, this worker of miracles, must die to preserve the nation, the religion, the church. Only thus could Israel be saved in the face of the riot that Rome would be sure to squelch. Caiaphas does not want God to be of service to Israel! He thinks he serves God. Well, is not that kind of service what it's all about? Hold the fort for God. Keep the Messiah's chair vacant and ready. We are God's people. We cut off this one Man and preserve the nation. We do God service.

Thus it was that Caiaphas prophesied more truly than he knew. Though his advice was from Satan, certainly, his words were the age-old words of the plan. He made his awful choice, and played into the hands of God. One would die for the people indeed, but how differently from the sinful plan of the high priest and all the priests and the Pharisees at the meeting that day who voted aye to Caiaphas' motion.

Choices Have to Be Made

The Passion story is the story of choices, choices presented by Satan to seduce into despair and other great shame and vice. Whatever his reasoning may have been, Judas had a choice. He carefully weighed Jesus against thirty pieces of silver, the going price for a slave, and chose the wrong treasure. He had the choice of leading the temple guard up some blind alley; he led them straight to Gethsemane and betrayed Jesus with a kiss. Peter had choice in the courtyard of the high priest's home to honor Jesus with loyalty; instead he took an oath, smashing the sacred commandment, and lied. Caiaphas had opportunity to change his approach when he presided at the last meeting of the Sanhedrin; he rose in indignation that Jesus should be guilty of blasphemy, and called for the vote that would sentence Jesus to the gallows.

Pilate had choice. He found Jesus innocent of the charges, no threat to Rome, yet he ordered Him scourged and allowed Him to be crucified. Pilate's was the choice between humoring the priests or the life of Jesus. The mob outside Pilate's porch were offered a choice, Barabbas, the arch-criminal or Jesus. For a few pennies they called for the arch-criminal and sent innocent Jesus to His death. Even the soldiers, faced with the choice of duty toward God or country, chose to keep their jobs, blaming it, as soldiers have always done, on their training to obey orders. One wonders, did the centurion who stood at the cross and spoke the only eulogy offered for Jesus, "This was a righteous Man and the Son of God," sleep well that night?

God Has Choices to Make

But choices are not limited to humans. God was faced with the choice of judgment or mercy when the first parents reached for the fruit of the tree of good and evil. Should He abandon man to damnation or devise a plan by which man might be saved eternally? In mercy, in love, from the depths of His God-nature, He chose to redeem man from his predicament through the visitation of His Son to the human family. The plan devised was one of substitution. Let My Son be substitute for man under judgment. Let Him alone suffer for the sin of the world. It is expedient for one Man to die for the people . . . if that One is the Son of God. Jesus summed it all up for Nicodemus one night on a rooftop. "God so loved the world that He gave His only begotten Son. . . ."

Jesus faced choices, too. To step into the Jordan River required decision, for, having taken that step, the course toward the cross was set. By identifying Himself with sinners, He made solemn declaration that He would die for them. Satan came to Him with choices in the wilderness temptations: bread for the body or the Word for the soul! security in the Father's love by testing it, or trust in the Father's concern in spite of the tragedy the future would bring; the Kingdom ushered in by bowing to Satan or by way of the cross. It took courage to set His face toward Jerusalem, to face His accusers, to hear their sentences of death, to endure the cross. He could have made other choices even on the cross, as those on crucifixion hill that day called out to Him, "If you are the Son of God, save Yourself and us." But Jesus had said yes to the Father, His yes to the world, His yes to us. Every choice He made, though it took Him day by day and step by step toward hell, was made because He would be obedient to His Father, to the plan, and to His love for us.

And Still Divine Choices

There is another process of choosing. The Passover was at hand, and by the ancient divine decrees, lambs had to be selected for the Passover meal and the Passover sacrifices at the temple. People would soon be swarming into the city of Jerusalem to mark proper religious observance of the Holy Days. Lambs and sheeps, ready to meet the needs of the feast, were even now being herded into the city for sale to the townspeople and the teeming multitude who would soon be arriving in the city. Choose your lamb for the Passover. It must be of a proper size and weight; it must be without spot or blemish. It is to be an offering to Jahweh God.

Already the priests have sharpened their knives, for the animals must be killed in the approved manner. They were the connoisseurs of the sheep. Just now they were meeting in solemn conclave in the board room of the temple. All unwittingly, they were choosing a lamb, the Lamb, for the slaughter. The choice is the high priest's. "It is expedient for one Man to die for the people": this is the Lamb who will expiate the sins of the people. This is the Lamb we will spear upon the spit and set in the fires of hell. This is our Passover Lamb. "Father, forgive them, they know not what they do."

In heaven, the Father (if we may speak of Him in human terms) hides His face. Christ Jesus is His only begotten Son, in whom He is well pleased, and precisely because He is, the affairs on earth are moving to their awesome climax. It may help to imagine the tension in heaven. If one remembers the Abraham-Isaac story. Father Abraham moved slowly up the mountain which God had shown him. Isaac, carrying the materials for the fire walked beside him. "Where is the lamb we will offer, father," Isaac wanted to know. "God will provide," replied the father. They came to the plateau and set up the altar. Abraham bound his only son hand and foot after the manner of binding animals for sacrifice. He gently laid him on the altar and was quite prepared to slay his son. When one walks beside Abraham, thinks his thoughts, and experiences the emotion tearing at his heart, he is almost overcome by the awesome test to which Abraham had been put. Transfer the scene to heaven, as the Father watches the events below. Yet He can and will do nothing to reverse the events going on in the temple. The Father had choices to make, too, and He chooses to remain silent, to let Caiaphas have his way. The Father's choice?—His Son or the world. God so loved the world that He gave up to die—His beloved Son. But our imagination is limited by our finiteness. The choice, the problem, the suffering in heaven is on a God-scale, so vast, so profound, so removed that we can at best only guess at it.

God's Choices Benefit Us

God's Son has taken the sin of the world into His own body on the tree; He has taken upon Himself all of God's wrath and judgment. And now God offers us His pardon for Jesus' sake. Reject Christ and face the consequences of your sin. Accept Him and receive full pardon. Which will it be for you? Receive God's gift, and then make your choices for God. Make every thought, every word, every situation work for Christ. How can I think this thought, speak such a word, or act so—and sin against God? The children of God, strive to think and speak and act so that their lives conform to the pattern set by Jesus Himself. Like children learning to walk, they stumble, they fall; but by the grace and generosity of God, they rise in God's rich forgiveness, praying that choices matching their faith be made. Having received Christ, they would not dishonor Him with unrighteous living.

Meanwhile

Before the temple conclave was over, the conversation turned to the possibility of Jesus showing up for the Passover feast. A motion was made and quickly passed that anyone knowing His whereabouts should report to the authorities, that Jesus might be taken into custody. From that moment on He was a marked Man. The hour of God had come. His baptism in our stead lay just before Him.

Events moved quickly after that. On the eve of the triumphal procession into Jerusalem Jesus dined with Mary, Martha, and Lazarus. During dinner Mary annointed Jesus' feet with precious ointment. Judas, as one might expect, objected to such a waste of costly perfume, but Jesus saw Mary's concern as a special sign of His impending death. "Against the day of My burying hath she done this," He explained. The next morning, Jesus, the Man marked for death, presented Himself to the city. The question of His attending the Passover had its answer. Jesus had made Himself available to courts and to the cross. No, more than that, He had made Himself available to the judgment of God and hell!

Judas negotiated with the chief priest to betray His whereabouts and collected the bounty. They arrested Him in the Garden of Gethsemane. They hauled Him to three different tribunals. They, to all appearances, won the day when they saw Him hanging from the tree. They were sure of it when they watched Him carried into the tomb. Just to be certain, they saw to it that the tomb stone was sealed with the imperial seal of Rome. Caiaphas' prophecy had been fulfilled: One Man had died for the people. The nation, Jewry, was safe. Weary to the bone, Caiaphas went home. He had done God service that day.

Caiaphas did do God service, but little did he know the service he did. One Man had died for the people, but on such a scale that Caiaphas' parochial concern pales into insignificance. In that one Man, the nefarious choices of the high priest and the choice of the most high God converge—that the world might be redeemed, the kingdom of God be established, and the mansions prepared for mankind might be filled. "God so loved the world that He gave up His only begotten Son that whosoever believeth in Him should not perish [in hell], but have everlasting life." Amen.

Reaction

Scripture Readings: Matthew 27:27-44; 1 Peter 2:17-25;
Psalm 22

Text: Matthew 27:39-44

When at last the suffering, death, and resurrection of Jesus were over, St. Paul could write his thrilling truth that "so many of us as were baptized into Jesus Christ were baptized into His death" (Rom. 6:3). God, the theologians say, sees us as living in the 20th century, but telescoped into the 1st, so that we are identified, as it were, as suffering, dying, and being buried together with Christ by our baptism. Small wonder that Christians through the ages have made dramatic ritual of Baptism. In many places and at various times people have gathered at the river. The candidates renounced the world for Christ and were lowered beneath the water to symbolize the death of the baptismal candidate. He was then lead by his new Christian brothers and sisters to the opposite bank to be dressed in a white robe, a symbol of his new life in Christ.

"Therefore we are buried with Him by baptism into death; that like as Christ was raised . . . by the glory of the Father, even so we also should walk in the newness of life" (Rom. 6:4). Because of His death (through which we pass in Baptism), our sins are forgiven, we are marked with the guarantee of the Holy Spirit, we are confirmed in the priesthood, we are initiated into the body of Christ. None of this could or would be true had Christ not died for us. Christian baptism gains its authenticity and power because of Christ's death in our stead.

No Relief

Jesus was never allowed to deviate from the path that led to the cross. His baptism, in which He identified Himself with sinners, tells us that. His healing miracles tell us that. To the man sick of the palsy He said, "Your sins are forgiven you; take up your bed and walk." The man's sins could not be forgiven without the cross! As surely as Jesus said His healing word, so surely He must go to the cross. Blind Bartimaeus, the demon-possessed lad; Jairus' daughter, whom He raised from the dead; Lazarus—each is a signal to anyone who reads the Sacred Record that Jesus would die, must die; for the healing necessitated forgiveness, and forgiveness comes to us only through the cross. As the crowds came to Him and He healed all manner of diseases, He sealed His destiny.

There is no relief for Jesus. He came into Jerusalem in a triumphant processional, riding on a donkey. The crowds shouted their hosannas and cried their blessing and hailed Him as their King. St. Luke puts the whole affair into perspective. They "began to rejoice and praise God with a loud voice for all the mighty works that they had seen," he writes (Luke 19:37 KJV). In such an observation, and Jesus was surely aware of it, all the triumph of the occasion is deflated. The people saw the miracles; they praised Jesus. They didn't see the Anointed One, the Christ, who did them. There is little joy in Jesus' heart on that first procession of the palms.

Jesus prayed in Gethsemane for hours. Like Jacob of old He wrestled with God. "Take this cup from Me, nevertheless, not My will but Thine be done." We count on prayer to be answered; Jesus surely expected the Father to say Him yes. But an angel came to Him in His agony and brought Him the Father's answer. The answer was no.

Pilate's wife slept fitfully the night before the trial. She awoke in horror to find her dream had taken on reality. She sent word to Pilate immediately. "Have thou nothing to do with that just Man." But she was more concerned about her husband, whose political future was at stake, than ever she was about Jesus.

There is no relief in Simon of Cyrene, who carried the cross for Jesus out the Way of Sorrows. A soldier saw Simon there, muscles bulging. With the tip of his spear he prodded Simon toward the stumbling Jesus. "Him they compelled to bear the cross." So Simon carried Jesus' cross, but not out of love or compassion. He was forced into service. One didn't argue with the Roman soldiers.

There was no relief for Jesus. They fixed Him to the cross and raised Him against the sky. "Father, forgive them for they know not what they do." What a Savior! He had five words he might have used for "forgive." He chose to use the one that meant, "Hold back Your judgment against these men until I have redeemed them." The word meant the complete removal of the cause of the offense—which could not happen until the vicarious and propitiatory sacrifice of Christ had been accomplished. His prayer required His death.

We have affirmed that for Christ to be baptized meant to die. Or to put it the other way around, His death is, in truth, His baptism. For us baptism is a great and happy, albeit, moving, event. We have written our liturgies to surround Baptism with songs, with prayers, with the reading of Scripture. It was not so at Christ's "baptism." If there were prayers, He prayed them. If there were Scriptures, He quoted them. But if there were songs, the people sang them.

Liturgy for a Baptism

"They that passed by reviled Him, wagging their heads" and mocking Him. The Christ who prayed for them, the Christ who even now was redeeming them for whom He had prayed, became target of crude jokes, sheer blasphemy. This was the liturgy for Him and His baptism.

Who started it? It is no matter. From somewhere on the edge of the crowd, the chief priests, with the scribes and elders, wagged their heads in His direction, and called out in tones of dripping sarcasm,

"He saved others; Himself He cannot save . . . He trusted in God; let Him deliver Him now if He will have Him. For He said, 'I am the Son of God.' " (Matt. 27:42-43 KJV)

Poor priests, poor scribes, you have the facts clean and clear. He indeed said, "I am the Son of God," and you wouldn't believe. Yes, He saved others. Yes, He could save Himself. And He is saving you from this mocking, from this murder, from hell. You mean you didn't hear His prayer for you, "Father, forgive them." He meant you, poor deluded priest, poor damned elder. Repent now—and believe.

Now the rulers, taking their cue from the priests and the elders, deride Him. With a thumb jabbed in the general direction of the cross, they passed the mocking cry of the priests on.

"He saved others," they cried to the crowd at the foot of the cross, "Let Him save Himself, if He be the Christ, the Chosen of God." (Luke 23:35 KJV)

There was laughter on the hill. Executions were a pleasant diversion. When a man says He is God, there is room for some choice and crude jokes, especially when His life ends like this. The rulers knew this, and they knew the temper of the kind of people who stopped to see a hanging. The priests had set the stone to rolling. The elders gave it momentum. Now the people push it on as they pick up the mockery and steer the "stone" directly at the cross.

The people wagged their heads (the record says) and reviled Him. Unlike the priests and the rulers, they stand more boldly in front of Him. They spread their legs and put their hands on their hips and unashamedly look at Him and wag their heads and revile Him:

"Thou that destroyest the temple and buildest it in three days, save Thyself. If Thou be the Son of God, come down from the cross. . . ." (Matt. 27:40 KJV)

The soldiers, looking for relief from the tedium of their duty and for some stay from the tension of the business they were engaged in, mock Him, too. They came to Him and offered Him vinegar to drink from a sponge at the end of a spear. The others kept their distance, but the soldiers were only a spear length away. They looked Him full in the face . . . and they found courage, even while they looked, to add their mocking taunts to Him.

"If Thou be the King of the Jews, save Thyself!" (Luke 23:37 KJV)

The stone rolls even closer as one of the malefactors which were hanged with Him railed on Him. How close to a prayer it is, and yet how far away, when the malefactor shouts across at Him. This close to salvation, all the words without the faith, for his prayer is not a prayer at all.

"If Thou be the Christ, save Thyself and us!" (Luke 23:39 KJV)

and you can hear him laugh in the midst of His pain.

"If Thou be . . ." the people passing by cried out. "If Thou be . . ." the reviling soldiers cried. "If Thou be . . ." the dying thief railed at Him. He offered no defense. His mission of the salvation of the world allowed Him no defense. Or . . . was His defense offered when they had nailed Him safely to the cross . . . in that prayer . . . "Father, forgive them. . . ."

But wait. The record tells us that His defense council hangs on the other cross at His side. One, at least, on the hill that day took stock and asked for mercy. The other thief, answering, rebuked his railing friend. "Dost not Thou fear God, seeing thou art in the same condemnation? And we indeed justly, for we receive the due reward of our deeds; but this Man has done nothing amiss." And he said to Jesus, "Lord, remember me when Thou commest into Thy kingdom." (Luke 24:40-42 KJV)

Jesus slowly turned His head to face the man who had uttered the first kind word to Him since the upper room, who in spite of appearances, or was it because of them, laid bare His heart, to reveal a tiny jewel of faith. Jesus speaks, with a "so be it," with a strong amen.

"Verily I say unto thee, today shalt thou be with Me in paradise!" (Luke 23:43 KJV)

For those who heard it, and will hear it, let this be said: Jesus was not coming down from the cross. Let the chorus of the mockers swell with point and counter melody, let them mock and rail as they will, let Satan direct the score as he will for this baptism, you cannot change the mind and will of our Jesus. Even though He spoke to a thief, He was announcing His intention to be faithful to the business of redeeming the world. He could not have made such a promise to the dying thief if He had any other intention. He is the soloist at His own baptism. His is the voice that soars above the chorus and sings the counter melody. The song the world chose to sing at His baptism, filled with dissonant sounds, is climaxed with His solo voice. "Today," the soloist's aria soars, "Today shalt thou be with Me in paradise."

The fearful day of the Lord reached high noon just then. A cloud moved across the heavens and blotted out the sun from horizon to horizon. The hill was in darkness. The nighttime at noon silenced the mocking crowd, the soldiers, the rulers, the priests. Now is the hour of the Father. Now He must hold His peace, too. He must stay His hand. He dare not speak the word that will spare His Son, for the salvation of the world He so loved depended on His willingness to sacrifice His only begotten Son.

This is the hour of the Prince of Darkness, of Satan. Satan has free rein. Job had more protection than Jesus. Of Job God had said, "His life you may not take." But the soul of the Prince of heaven is given without let or hindrance, to be twisted and tortured, bent and broken, in the hands of Satan. Do not let the silence or the darkness mislead you . . . not as far as Christ is concerned, for He had been delivered into the hands of Satan.

Who has ever made a choice like this? These are the alternatives for the Father: My beloved Son or the sin-stained people of the world. Like the mob that only a short time before had chosen Barabbas, so God the Father makes His choice. "This day, beloved Son, I abandon You and choose sinful mankind." No wonder, O Father, You hid Yourself from the Crucified One behind that darkened sun.

Commentary

The poets put it better than the essayist. Isaiah, in his great chapter from the Song of the Suffering Servant (53), may have spoken before the event in prophecy, but he couched the awful event in poet imagery:

> All we like sheep have gone astray; we have turned everyone to his own way; and the Lord hath laid on Him the iniquity of us all. (v. 6)

The poet king wrote the first Lenten hymn in Psalm 22. He speaks in imagery with poetic force.

> Be not far from Me; for trouble is near, for there is none to help. . . . I am poured out like water, and all My bones are out of joint: My heart is like wax; it is melted in the midst of My bowels. (Ps. 22:11, 14)

Or the poets of a later day, like Thomas Kelly, who wrote the hymn "Stricken, Smitten, and Afflicted." Hear him as he evaluates the meaning of the passion of Jesus.

> Ye who think of sin but lightly,
> Nor suppose the evil great
> Here may view its nature rightly,
> Here its guilt may estimate.
> Mark the Sacrifice appointed,
> See who bears the awful load;
> 'Tis the Word, the Lord's Anointed,
> Son of Man and Son of God.

Reactions

So the reactions set in one by one. The high priest resented the raising of Lazarus from the dead. He engineered the trial before the Sanhedrin, and almost to a man they reacted positively (for the high priest) to his call for the death of Jesus. Pilate acted positively to the high priest, too; for seeking favor with the people, he delivered Jesus to be crucified. The soldiers were trained to obedience, so that the order to take Jesus out to crucify Him was obeyed without question. The people heard the high priest's mockery, and chimed in without hesitation.

Jesus and the Father reacted in forgiving love. Jesus did not come down from the cross. The plan for man's salvation demanded His death, and He stayed on the cross to the end with His love, His prayer for the forgiveness of His tormentors, His promise to the thief—that all might be saved to the uttermost. Nor did the Father intervene in the affairs on the hill. Justice demanded the death penalty; love for humanity required that Jesus, His only begotten Son, pay it. As obscene as men were at the trial and on Calvary, the Father would not, could not, intervene.

The centurion reacted to it all. His is the last voice of which we have a record from the scene of Christ's crucifixion. "Surely this was a righteous man and the Son of God."

And we, we who stand to benefit so much by Jesus' baptism, what is our reaction to it all? Forgiveness starts there at Christ's "baptismal font," and then comes new life, and hope, and eternal glory. Perhaps now we ought to borrow the words of another poet, who wrote a refrain for his stanzas . . .

> Thousand, thousand thanks shall be,
> Dearest Jesus, unto Thee.

Amen.

The Sacrifice

Scripture Readings: Matthew 27:45-46; Matthew 18:21-35;
   Romans 7:14—8:3

Text: Matthew 27:45-46

Father Abraham was commanded by God to offer his only and beloved son Isaac as a sacrifice. Such was Abraham's fidelity to God that he took Isaac to the mountain, bound him as one bound a sacrificial animal, and was about to plunge the knife into Isaac when an angel intervened. At the moment interpretation of the Abraham story is not of concern. Whether it is prophetic of the sacrifice of Christ is here not the point. The reason for mentioning it at all is because we can identify with Abraham's feelings in the terrible testing through which God moved Him. Who has not shuddered each time he heard the story? How could God! How could Abraham!

Whatever else there is, there is parallelism between the Abraham story and the story of our redemption. While the human agents, Judas, for instance, and Caiaphas and Pilate and the others, move Jesus to the cross, it is the Father who, like Abraham, must watch the catastrophic events and, because He could not, would not intervene, suffers in divine dimensions what Abraham suffered in human dimensions. Abraham so loved God that he was willing to sacrifice his son. God so loves us that He was willing to give up His Son to death.

One senses a Father's pride (we are speaking anthropomorphically, that is, endowing God with human characteristics, the better to understand Him), as Jesus identified Himself with sinners when He stepped into the Jordan to be baptized. The Father broke His usual silence to address His Son quite audibly: "You are My beloved Son; with You I am well pleased." If there is "pride" in those words, there is far more, for they are the announcements of Jesus' destiny. His baptism in the sinners' baptism of John set Jesus squarely on the road to the cross. From this road He would not deviate, though the devil might seek to dissuade Him, though men might throw obstacles into His way. The

Father's heart surely (to use human terms again), surely must have skipped a beat, for He was sending His sinless Son to hell.

The meaning and import of Jesus' baptism never escaped Him. If the Son of God must redeem the world to fulfill the Father's love for sinful humanity, He would fulfill the trust the Father had placed in Him. Satan might tempt Him to short-cut the whole mission; He would fulfill His trust. Peter might try to dissuade Him at the transfiguration or at Caesarea Philippi; He would be faithful to the trust. James and John might make their bid for honored places in His kingdom. He, not they, would drink the cup and be baptized with the baptism that lay ahead. Let Him speak in the marketplace, the baptism that lay ahead of Him was on His mind. On at least one occasion He interrupted Himself to say: "I have a baptism to be baptized with; and how I am constrained until it is accomplished!" (Luke 12:50). He told a parable about a vineyard owner whose tenants murdered the owner's son when he came to collect the land fees. In due time He set His face toward Jerusalem, for the hour of His baptism, His sacrifice, was at hand.

He might have stayed the soldiers in Gethsemane when they came to arrest Him. He could have spoken in His own defense before Caiaphas and the Sandedrin. The angel of death might well have destroyed evil Herod, or killed the firstborn of the Romans to free Him from Pilate. But there was no way Jesus would let Himself be deterred.

With calculated efficiency they drove Him out of the circles of those whose moral duty it was to shelter Him. Caiaphas and the Sanhedrin excommunicated Him, the Son of God, on charges of blasphemy. The church was never more mistaken, never more vicious, than it was then. "We, the chosen people of God, have no use for You, Jesus of Nazareth." With a single voice they forced Him from the community of people who prided themselves on being the people of God.

One could expect evil actions like that of Herod. Yet Herod, as tetrach over Galilee, had moral responsibilities too, though it is doubtful if he ever exercised them. In his superstitious mind he imagined that John the Baptist, whom he had beheaded, had returned to haunt him. He demanded miracles. Jesus stood silent before him. Then in good politician's style, Herod hung a white toga on Him—the symbol of a political aspirant (Was he not charged with aspiration to Herod's throne?)—and sent Him back to Pilate. The nation, the government, has that responsibility, you know. It is given and designed to protect its own. But the nation that God had espoused for a thousand years declared Him an outlaw and sent Him to His death.

The human family, with all its squabbling, is a family still. Pilate stands as the family's representative. The clamor of the crowd at the pretorium porch, the insistence of the chief priests, prevailed. Pilate washed his hands of Jesus and allowed the death sentence. This day Jesus was declared the black sheep of the family. He must be purged from the family tree. When Pilate washed his hands, he thought himself slipping out from the responsibility of Jesus' death. No way could Pilate, whose one word would have set Jesus free, cleanse himself from the guilt of that day. Anatole France wrote a story in which Pilate, as he (according to tradition) lived out his life in the Swiss Alps to which he had been banished, is constantly washing imaginary stains from his fingers, as if mere washing could remove his guilty involvement. The death sentence has been spoken. The Lamb for the sacrifice had been carefully picked. Now, like Isaac who carried the faggots for the sacrifice at Mount Moriah, Jesus carried the wooden beam up the hill called Calvary.

They nailed Him to the cross, then. They pushed the cross up against the sky, and dropped it into the socket someone had dug to hold it. They mocked Him, using words as Satan had used them in the wilderness: "If You are the Son of God, save Yourself; come down from the cross. Assert Yourself and prove Your claim, and we will believe." He prayed for them then, that the Father would hold His judgment until the price—even for them—be paid. He spoke words of assurance to the repentant thief about His arrival in Paradise that very day. He set His household in order, there on the hill, as He commended His mother to John's safekeeping. Man had done his worst; Jesus had been excluded from all of mankind's communities. Alone, alone, He faced the Father's wrath; alone He faced our hell.

The Sacrifice

The sun burns bright and hot in the Near East. Activity ceases at noon, to avoid the high-noon heat. That day the noonday sun was blotted out by a cloud, by a darkness over all the land. "From the sixth hour there was darkness over all the land until the ninth hour," from high noon until three. It brought a certain relief to the people on the hill. The soldiers may well have appreciated the respite it brought. But it was ominous. It wasn't normal. Fear came upon them all. The mocking ceased, and quiet came to the hill. No ribald jests, no sarcastic barbs. Only quiet on the hill, broken only by the crucified ones gasping for breath.

The darkness is merciful. It hides beneath its cover the awesome events that are taking place this high noon of the awful day of the Lord. The darkness is fear-filled, for it is happening just at noon on the day of the Lord. Joel, the prophet, had anticipated it. "The sun and the moon are darkened, and the stars withdraw their shining. And the Lord roars from Zion, and utters His voice from Jerusalem, and the heavens and the earth shake" (Joel 3:15-16). And Isaiah prophesied it: "Behold, the day of the Lord comes, cruel, with wrath and fierce anger, to make the earth a desolation. . . . For the stars of heavens and their constellations will not give their light; the sun will be dark at its rising and the moon will not shed its light" (Is. 13:9-10).

In the darkness Christ steps, as it were, over the borderline between earth and hell, between heaven and hell. He is altogether under the judgment of God. He is abandoned by the Father—abandoned to hell. This, then, is where it all was to lead—His baptism at the Jordan where first He assumed the world's sin, the baptism with which He was constrained until it should come to pass, the abandonment by the church, the nation, the human family, and now by the Father. It has been said that Jesus was the loneliest man in all the history of the world—out there on the cross. Alone—He was delivered to Satan and to hell. Alone—He endured that which had been pronounced against the sinner by a righteous God. Alone—He was the substitute for all humanity, the substitute for you and me.

"You are My beloved Son." The Father said it. Now to be reconciled to the world, He abandons His beloved Son. No wonder He causes darkness at noon on this day. He cannot bear to look upon the Son whom He has abandoned. No wonder the cloud covered the land; the Son is not permitted so much as a ray of light from the heavens. "You are My beloved Son":—and He gives His Son into the hands of Satan and hell.

Bits and pieces of the puzzle of hell lie here and there in Scripture waiting to be fitted into the picture. Jesus' parable of the rich man and Lazarus tells that in hell the rich man lifted up his eyes to heaven and pleaded for a drop of water, for he was tormented in the flames of hell. The burnt offering, a sacrifice of a yearling lamb offered morning and evening in the temple, was the one offering in which the whole animal was burned for the forgiveness of sins. (It was, by the way, the one offering that could be made by a non-Israelite). The word that describes such an offering by fire is "holocaust." So, on the evening of the Passover, the Lamb of God is offered in a holocaust for the forgiveness of sins. It is indeed a baptism by fire, the supreme holocaust, the ultimate baptism for the remission of the sin of the world.

How judiciously Matthew covers the terror of the most cataclysmic event in the world's history in a few words: "Now from the sixth hour there was darkness over all the land until the ninth hour." In the cover of that "darkness over all the land" the plan, devised in the Trinitarian councils, was consummated. Its implications are greater than our finite imagination, but even our imagination devises pictures enough to help

42

us appreciate the love wherewith we are loved by the Father and the Son, One willing to abandon, the other ready to be abandoned—for us. The Father willing to give up His Son—to hell; the Son willing to go to hell, to be a stranger in the realms of the Prince of Darkness, in the name of justice, for the rebellious world—for me. Do not, ever, underestimate the cry from the cross as the three dread hours drew to their end: "My God, My God, why hast Thou forsaken Me?" They are words that speak of the terror of hell.

The light, the sun, came back again. The time of darkness and hell was finished. He cried for water to moisten His tongue, cleaving to His jaws. He announced to earth, and hell and heaven, that it was over. "It is finished!" He cried. Hell heard Him say it, and heaven. Through those who heard it on the hill that afternoon, it is there for all the world to hear. Christ has been baptized with the baptism wherewith we could not be baptized. Then, in the waning afternoon, He commended His Spirit to His Father, as One victorious in the strife, and died. The plan, devised at the fall of man, by which sinful humanity might stand again before God and life, had been carried out. God so loved the world that He gave up to the holocaust His only-begotten and well-beloved Son!

After the Sacrifice

The subsequent story is the story of Easter and the resurrection of Jesus from death and the grave. On the third day He rose again. His temple riddle, for which the chief priest labeled Him blasphemous and demanded His death, and which the people on Calvary hurled at Him with mocking voices, was resolved. He appeared to Mary, to Peter, to the Emmaus disciples, to Thomas. He ascended into heaven, leaving behind Him His mandate to baptize in the name of the Father, the Son, and the Holy Spirit. On Pentecost, at the outpouring of the Spirit, the first Christian baptisms took place, with 3,000 people availing themselves of Christ's baptism. Christ's baptism, accomplished for all people in the darkness of Calvary, had passed over into Christian baptism .

Only when the plan had been completed, only when Christ had died and risen again, could St. Paul write the amazing truth that by Baptism we die with Christ, we are buried with Christ, we rise with Christ, we live with Christ. Only now could Peter make the assertion that "Baptism . . . now saves you . . . through the resurrection of Jesus Christ" (1 Peter 3:21). It is from our Lord's baptism that our baptism draws its meaning, its purpose, and its power. Had there been no cross, there could be no Christian baptism.

Luther puts it all into good perspective in his explanation of Baptism. "What does Baptism give or profit?" he asks, and then supplies the answer. "It works forgiveness of sins" (possible only after the cross), "delivers from death and the devil" (made possible only by the cross), "and gives eternal salvation" (the prime, the ultimate blessing of the cross), "to all who believe this" (faith is a gift of the Holy Spirit), "as the words and promises of God declare."

It is from the baptism of Jesus, including the supreme offering for the sin of the world, and ours, that we through our baptism are reconciled to God, find peace again with God, dare to stand before God, and have burning in us the hope of the life to come. Do not underestimate the meaning of your baptism for you and God's people. By the grace of Jesus Christ it has taken you from the realm of the Prince of Darkness into the family of the living God.

The centurion in general charge of the death penalties that fateful day carried out his orders with indifference. He dared not get involved with the criminals who deserved capital punishment, much less with the validity of the court that had decreed such judgment. This Jesus of Nazareth, King of the Jews, though, was different from anyone he had crucified before. No one had ever prayed when he was being crucified. Never had there been such darkness during a crucifixion. He couldn't get that cry: "Eli, Eli, lama sabachthani?" out of his mind, or that prayer at the end of it all just before He died: "Father, into Thy hands I commit My spirit." Only one conclusion fit this Man. The centurion drew the right conclusion, as he made his commentary: "Truly, this was the Son of God!" Amen.

Maundy Thursday

Covenant

Scripture Readings: Genesis 2:15-17; Exodus 19:4-6;
Matthew 26:26-29

Text: Matthew 25:26-29

In the night in which our Lord was betrayed, He quietly exercised His
privilege to fellowship for the last time with the Twelve by celebrating
the Seder meal with them as the Passover time drew near. There was so
much to say, and so little time in which to say it. The great servant role
His disciples were to exercise after He was gone must be emphasized.
The deep necessity of faith and trust in Him, if the servant role was to be
maintained, needed one last restatement. He must sound again the call
to love—to love enough to die for each other or for Him if the need
should arise. He must pray for them and the whole great mission to
which He was committed and to which they must commit themselves.
So much to do; so little time.

When at last the roasting of the lamb, center for the Passover meal,
was finished, they arranged themselves about the table. Whether
anyone asked the age-old question: "Why do we celebrate this night
above all others?" to begin the traditional Passover commemoration,
Scripture does not mention. Yet the prescribed ritual must surely have
been followed. They drank the first cup of wine, remembering the great
promise of Yahweh: "I will bring them out," and the hope that His
promise had kindled in the slaves of Egypt. They drank a second cup, as
the recital of the liberating history continued, when they came to the
second promise: "I will deliver you from bondage." The traditional
third cup was drunk at the words: "I will redeem you."

It is here, it is believed, that Jesus took the bread and blessed it, and
gave it to them, saying: "Take, eat; this is My body." And it is here that
He took the cup of wine, drank a swallow of it Himself, and handed it to
them, saying: "Drink of it, all of you; for this is My blood of the
covenant, which is poured out for many for the forgiveness of sins." The
loaf passed about the table; each of them broke off a portion and ate,

45

wondering about this strange addition to the ancient rituals. The cup, too, passed from hand to hand and mouth to mouth, as they all drank of it, perplexed, no doubt, at His words and what they might mean.

The moment passed, and the meal continued. The fourth and last cup, the one poured at the words, "I will take you for My people," was drunk, and the thoughts of those about the table that night were strangely disturbed. Jesus gave no extended explanation (that we know of) for the interpolation at the third cup. The hour grew late. In a moment He must leave. He called for the traditional hymns, a portion of the Psaltery, and they sang together as good religious folk do. When the sound of the men's deep voices ended, He arose from the table and they began to leave. Jesus moved down the steps, out into the narrow street, down the long hill toward Gethsemane and the cross. What He had just done He did in anticipation of the Gethsemane prayers, the devastating trial, the pain of the cross, and above all the terrifying judgment demanded to fulfill His portion of the covenant He had made with them over a broken loaf and a cup of wine. Without His suffering and death there would be no remission of sin, no new covenant by which and in which to live with Him.

When at last the divine mission to redeem mankind from its sin and the multitude of sinners from perdition had been accomplished, when the resurrection was an assured fact and the hour for His departure had come, He gathered His disciples on the hill of the Ascension and commanded them to go into the world to teach and to baptize all nations. For His followers Baptism would be forever the sign of repentance, of faith and commitment, of initiation into the Kingdom, of ordination to the royal priesthood, of dedication to His mission of bringing the nations to the knowledge of what He did for all people.

On Pentecost 3,000 souls were baptized. From that moment and from that place the proclamation of the Good News in Jesus Christ was carried into Judea and "to the end of the earth." Everywhere His followers went, they taught and baptized. The Kingdom, like a mustard seed, germinated and grew, until like a mustard plant in which the birds of the air might nest, it became a resting place for masses of people. As the Kingdom expanded, the followers of Jesus remembered the night in the upper room when He had instituted the new covenant in His body and blood. The implications of what Jesus had meant by the bread and the wine, and the words that accompanied them, took on greater meaning, giving additional strength and purpose to the gift He had left them.

"Do this in remembrance of Me," He had said. Celebration of the Sacred Meal is a feast of remembrance. Whenever it has been celebrated, it has recalled the night in which He was betrayed into the

46

hands of evil men and allowed to suffer and die by a just God. One who communes is reminded and reassured of forgiveness and the purchase price so dearly paid for him or her. "Until . . . I drink it new with you in My Father's kingdom," He said, and Christians have joyously anticipated the feast in glory when they will celebrate with Him in the mansions above.

And in the here and now, between the past and the future, the celebration of the Supper takes on meaning for baptized Christians. It becomes for them the constant reinforcement of their baptismal commitment. Baptism is a one-time event; the celebration of the body and the blood is an ever-recurring event and a constant reminder of goals and purposes to which they were set at their baptism.

Baptism is, for instance, initiation into the body of Christ (1 Cor. 12:13). The Lord's Supper strengthens the unity of Christ's followers, "so that the world may believe that Thou hast sent Me" (John 17:21). The unity of the community is nowhere more clearly manifested than in the moment of intimate and profound communion at the Lord's table, for the celebration of the Sacrament has not only the vertical dimension (one to One) but a horizontal dimension (one to all) as well. Here in this moment the whole world, if it bothers to look, can see the bond of love that binds Christians to each other in Christ.

Baptism confers the priesthood (1 Peter 2:9; the phrase "out of darkness into His marvelous light" is synonymous with baptism). The priesthood confers privileges and responsibilities. It offers the privilege of the Throne Room of God for prayer and thanksgiving and praise. It grants access to the presence of God, as an emissary has access to the king's private chambers. It carries responsibilities. Priests are at the disposal of the king; so all baptized people are at the disposal of the King, of Christ, of God. Thus, while they enjoy their privileges, they must be duly aware of their responsibilities. It is so easy to forget, to neglect, to find excuses when it comes to carrying out the King's mission to the world. The Supper reminds them of who they are through Baptism and reconstitutes them for the tasks to which they have been assigned in the world. The Supper recalls the past ("in remembrance"), anticipates the future ("until He comes"), and gives security to His followers to live and work in freedom in the present.

There is a similarity between the baptism of our Lord at the Jordan and our own. Jesus stepped into the sinners' baptism of John the Baptist, and thus identified Himself with those acknowledged sinners whom John baptized. Yet He was without sin and quite without the need of John's baptism. He accepted it—and thus identified His purpose. His course was set—toward the cross and the fearful judgment of God against sin. His baptism and His mission cannot be separated. Our baptism has parallel implications. Through it we are identified with Christ. Though we are sinners still, the righteousness of Christ becomes ours. "We were buried with Christ by baptism into death," writes St. Paul (Rom. 6:4). We emerge from our baptism to serve God, that is, new purpose is given to life through Baptism, a new course is set. The Supper is Christ's gift to us to encourage and strengthen us in the life and living to which our baptism has committed us.

The Covenant

There in the upper room that night of betrayal, Jesus offered the New Covenant (from which our New Testament gets its name) to all who should come to Him. Through the Old Testament, into the New, God is a covenanting God. He made a covenant with Adam, for instance, conditioning the joys of Eden with the prohibition against eating of the tree of good and of evil. He covenanted with Abraham, not only promising him that he should be the father of many nations but that through his progeny the nations of the earth would be blessed. He covenanted with Israel at Mt. Sinai, speaking through His servant Moses: "If you will obey My voice and keep My covenant, you shall be My own possession among all peoples; for all the earth is Mine, and you shall be to Me a kingdom of priests and a holy nation" (Ex. 19:5-6). Take note of the "if" in God's words, for it marks this covenant as conditional. The terms require Israel to be faithful to the Ten Commandments. The whole Old Testament is the history of Israel's concern—or lack of it—for this Sinai covenant. It is the tower to which all history and the prophets are oriented. Israel proved unfaithful, and God determined to abrogate the Old and establish a New Covenant.

In the midst of the Passover meal, on that fateful night, Jesus took the bread and the wine to make it the sign of the New Covenant in His holy body and blood. The "condition" of the Old was removed. He took it upon Himself to reconcile the world to God by His passion and death, to make grace and forgiveness a free gift, to change obedience under law to servanthood in freedom. There are no strings, no "ifs," no conditions to the New Covenant. The Christian life is lived in Christ's forgiveness, in love, in appreciation.

No wonder, indeed, that the Sacrament to be celebrated in remembrance of Him should carry the Covenant to us. He knew our frailty. He understood the power of our sinful natures, the subtlety of Satan, the relentless call of the world. He knew the struggle life would demand of His followers, how often (like Paul) they would want to do the right thing and do the wrong, how many times they would struggle to live up to His example of loving and forgiving, how often they would let opportunities to be priests and servants slip by. He would stand behind them, still loving, still forgiving. He would be in the blessed Sacrament, remitting their sins, strengthening them, uniting them. The Holy Spirit would be there, putting the power to renew faith into the Word and the Sacrament. God would send us on our way again, in the power of the Spirit, to be lights and servants to the world. The New Covenant contains no "ifs," no conditions—only the superb promises of His faithfulness. Yet by it, in response to our Christ whom it calls anew to mind, we are impelled to live and, if need be, to die for Him.

Our Baptism, Our Covenant

This night we have come together to celebrate the Sacrament. We are a family, a community. Ours is "one Lord, one faith, one baptism, one God and Father of us all" (Eph. 4:5-6). This is our common denominator; it is this that binds us, disparate as we may be, into oneness in Christ. Then too, we are all sinners. And we are all priests, sharing the responsibility of priests to be at God's disposal. We are soldiers and servants of Christ.

By thought, word, and deed we have all failed our King. He will touch us all with His healing forgiveness and love in the blessed Sacrament. Renewed, we as one face the world again. We are oriented to the joy and responsibility of our baptism. We are His, and He is ours.

Amazing grace! Though the darkest of dark clouds gathered on Christ's horizon that night in which He was betrayed, He took time to think of us and our 20th-century needs. That is why, in grace and love, He covenanted with us and gave us the sign and seal of bread and wine, body and blood, in the New Covenant. That is why, in that fear-filled night, He took the bread and wine, blessed them, and gave them to us, saying: "This bread, this cup is broken and poured for you, and you, and you. It is My covenant with you, and you, and you, that this day's and all days' sins are forgiven and you are free to be My beloved sisters and brothers." Amen.

Good Friday

Children of the Heavenly Father

Scripture Readings: Hebrews 4:14-16; 5:7-10; Mark 15:33-39;
John 19:28-42

Text: John 19:30

On this holy evening, this solemn Good Friday, I would speak to you of the family of the heavenly Father and how it came to be, for it is on this day of days that impediments to our adoption into His family were removed. We are "children of the heavenly Father" only because of what happened on this day so long ago, when the only-begotten Son of the Father accomplished what He had come to do to make our adoption possible. That is why I have chosen to speak to you from this text. It is Christ's announcement—to the Father and the Holy Spirit, to Satan and all his evil angels, and to the whole human family—that the mission to save the world *from* perdition and *for* the heavenly Father was accomplished. Now a new creation, a family for God, as it were, was possible.

On this holy day, at three o'clock, Jesus died. Whatever an observer might have found and pieced together about the indecision of Pilate and the hatred and envy of the religious leaders, it would not be enough to justify what had taken place this day, and certainly not enough to explain it. Had such an observer been a witness to the crucifixion and death, he would not have been satisfied with what he had found, not, that is, if he had heard that cryptic utterance in the darkness and noticed that just at that moment the first rays of the afternoon sun had returned to dispel the noonday darkness.

Jesus had called for water. His tongue, as the psalmist sang so long before, "cleaved to His jaws." He could barely speak the word. A soldier fixed a sponge to a spear, dipped it in vinegar, and held it to His lips. Bitter as it was, it freed His tongue. He could speak clearly. Jesus strained to raise His head, His eyes, toward heaven. "It is finished!" He cried. And with that, St. John says, He bowed His head and gave up His spirit. "It is finished!" The moment was too fraught with emotion, with

50

pathos, with drama to ask questions just then. Or the minutes were too filled with feverish activity as they broke the legs of the thieves and thrust the spear into Jesus' side, a *coup de grace* just in case He was not dead. But the statement and the questions were there. If someone wanted to dig a little deeper into the reason and meaning of this cry, he must at least ask the questions: "Why did He say, 'It is finished'? What did He mean, 'It is accomplished'? To whom was He saying it, and why?"

"It"

Questions like these bring the moment of the cry, the announcement, into sharp focus. More than that, they bring the whole scene on Skull Hill into view. Something accomplished there in the darkness? Something completed in a crucifixion? Something finished by death? Ah, the scope of that little word. Into it must be poured so many things—the "fill-ful-ment" of prophecy, for instance. Jesus had come to fill the prophecies full of meaning. Now the promises to the primal pair were accomplished. Now the promises to Father Abraham were fulfilled. Now the ancient poem of King David (Psalm 22), written so long before the fact, had become a reality. Now the song of the prophet Isaiah, undecipherable for long centuries, was at last interpreted. Now God, who had long promised redemption, was vindicated. All that is accomplished.

Reconciliation is accomplished, reconciliation with God. The terrible and terrifying rift between God and sinner has been bridged. The substitution of God's only-begotten Son under the judgment of God to suffer the sinners' hell has been successfully accomplished. Now the Father's yearning for His beloved world, His desire that all mankind be saved from perdition, was guaranteed relief. The possibility of citizenship in the Kingdom for everyone awaited only the outpouring of the Holy Spirit. Allegiance to the Father by love, rather than by coercion, was in order, and God could now be Father to all who, like the prodigal son, would turn and come home. All that is accomplished.

The mission is finished. Dying is still to come, but that comes of itself. The mission is finished. The Word, Jesus the Christ, had become flesh to live among us. The Word had made the Father known. The Word had bowed to the Father's judgment and become obedient to death by the cross. The Word was in mission, sent from the Godhead to redeem the world, and by that redemption to call together a family for God. Now, at the ninth hour, at three o'clock, the mission was accomplished. The Word, the only-begotten and beloved Son of God, returned from hell. Freedom from the law and the wrath of God, from sin and death, is available to all who by faith in Jesus Christ will accept

51

the substitution. All this is involved in that little, all-embracing word "It."

"Is Finished!"

"It is finished!" The tense of the verb is in the present perfect. The victory announcement is an accomplished fact. The import of the announcement is clear. The action, the accomplishment, is done. The reason for the mission and the end of the mission has come in the lifting of the darkness and the coming of the light. Set the words in neon lights; shout the fact from the housetops; assign it prime time on the agenda! The redemption of the world is accomplished! Reconciliation of God to man is a perfected fact. The deep gulf between sinners and a just God has been bridged. Crucified thief, today you will be with Him in Paradise. Soldiers, tormenters, chief priests, Pilate, Herod, the Father will forgive you now. Palsied man, blind Bartimaeus, your sins are forgiven. The Son of God who came seeking sinners has destroyed the enemy, and in Him you have been found, in Him you are free.

The sour wine mixed with gall had freed the Savior's tongue. He raised His voice to heaven. He cried: "It is finished!" The announcement is made by God to God. This is God calling to God. This is the Son and Servant speaking to the Father. The word is meant for God. Even as it is spoken, the rustle of angel wings is heard again in heaven, and the Father, filled with agony during those three eternal hours, has bestirred Himself. It is the announcement for which He has been waiting. Now it has come and heaven can rejoice. The mission has come to a successful conclusion. Christ claimed the victory and, according to John, even as He claimed the victory He yielded up His life.

Satan, too, heard the word and cringed. The hour of his power was over. Before long He would be bound and cast forever into the bottomless pit. And people heard it. While it needed pondering in the minds and hearts of human beings, through the wisdom granted by the Holy Spirit they came to understand it. In the understanding came the wondrous peace of sinners forgiven through the intervention of God's beloved Son. A new vision was born as people came to appreciate the enormity of the word from the cross, one that had to do with what they were and who they are because God so loved them. A new and thrilling hope swept in with those words, the hope of eternal glory, of the Father's mansions, of life with God in time and for all eternity. "It is finished!" Perfect tense! New life! Life with and for and in God! Mission accomplished!

Children of the Heavenly Father

From this awesome moment, the promises of old became a reality. Through the accomplished mission of Jesus Christ, the metaphors He had so often delighted in took form and substance. The Shepherd, our Lord Jesus, gave His life for the sheep, and we, who live by faith in Him, have become His flock. We who once were aliens and foreigners have become citizens of the kingdom of God. We who once were no people have now become the people of God, the family gathered by the Holy Spirit for our Abba Father. Our Brother, by our adoption into the family of God, is He whom the voice at the baptism in the Jordan and on the mountain of the Transfiguration declared to be the Father's beloved Son, with whom He was well pleased. We are, by faith, all brothers and sisters in the family of God—children, indeed, of the heavenly Father.

Amazing truth that God should look at us through Jesus Christ, and love us as a dear Father loves His children. Amazing truth that He should nourish and cherish, love and console us, bear us in time, and carry us at last to the family mansions. Amazing truth that we can hear Him say of us: "These are my beloved sons and daughters." More amazing still, that we can hear the gracious invitation standing clear and certain at the end of John's vision and of our Scripture: "Come. And let him that is athirst come" (Rev. 22:17 KJV). Remembering that awesome, wondrous day, that first Good Friday so long ago, that terrible and terrifying darkness, and the mighty word from the cross, all God's children have accepted the invitation and are on their way to the marriage feast of the Lamb in glory. Amen.

You Are My Beloved Children

Sermons
for
the Sundays of
Lent Through Pentecost
by George M. Bass

Created as Children of God

Genesis 2:7-9, 15-17; 3:1-7 (longer lesson—Genesis 1—3)

Lent begins with a gathering of the people of God who have responded to the call to begin the discipline of what the church has called the "paschal season." Lent ends with a climb to Calvary, the contemplation of the crucified Christ, and the culmination of the Lord's death in the wonder and mystery of His resurrection-victory on the third day. Lent is the annual pilgrimage of God's people to the cross and the empty tomb of the risen Lord. It is a time for learning about the depths of Christ's suffering in preparation for the celebration of new life—a new creation—Easter Sunday and during Eastertide.

The famous shrine of St. Anne de Beaupre is an interesting place to visit. The "old" church has become a museum filled with artifacts—wheelchairs, crutches, canes, and braces—that testify to miraculous healings that purportedly have taken place there. The complex also contains a diorama, a building that enables visitors to stand on a platform and "circle" the walls of Jerusalem to see how it might have looked when Jesus was born. A replica of the Scala Sancta, the holy stairs of Pilate's judgment hall, is also there. A steep hill forms a backdrop for the shrine—with a pathway carved back and forth to the top. The Stations of the Cross are built into the path, each with almost life-size statuary depicting Christ's awful march to Calvary. At the top of the hill is a cross with the crucified Christ nailed to it. Beyond is a sort of Pieta, with Mary cradling her dead Son—and beyond that is the tomb. Finally, there is a representation of the empty tomb on Easter morning. One almost expects to hear one of the ancient Easter hymns:

> Behold, the stone is rolled away,
> And shining ones have come to say,
> "He is not here, but is risen!"
> The night of death is past and gone,
> Arise and greet the glorious morn,
> "He is not here, but is risen!"

Lent, for many of us, is simply following the pathway of Jesus' passion and suffering to Golgotha in an attempt to understand the need for the crucifixion, to mourn at His death, and to celebrate the Resurrection on Easter. We travel that path through penitential worship and devotions and daily prayer. It is a time to reflect on our own spiritual condition and repent of our sins as we seek again the reassurance that they are forgiven. Since the first centuries of Christian history, Lent has been more than this; it has been a time to remember and review the experience of God and His people. And so there was a time when the Old Testament lessons were read in public worship to retell the story from the beginning to the cross and the tomb of Christ—and find new meaning in the fuller story. Finally, the church selected 12 of these lessons and used them on Holy Saturday prior to the Sacrament of Baptism, which, with the Easter Communion, personalizes the "story of salvation" for each of us. Six of those lessons have been chosen to give content and shape to our Sunday experience this Lententide; they tell us that we are God's "beloved children," as they take us to and into the tomb with Christ and into new life. Lent observed this way becomes an opportunity to remember and renew our relationship with God and each other through Holy Baptism.

Lent will have more meaning and significance when we move through the stories of God and His people. We may discover that these are our stories, too, and that our involvement in them and their resolution in Christ's death and resurrection is in Holy Baptism. Perhaps we will be able to join Luther with an "I am baptized" as we ponder the Passion and celebrate the resurrection of our Lord on Easter Day. Perhaps we can find new meaning in the Gospel for our lives.

Lent Began in a Garden

A tragedy occurred among the trees of the garden—not the Garden of Gethsemane on the night that Jesus was betrayed and arrested, but in the Garden of Eden. The Lord God created Adam and Eve as the final act in the drama of Creation, and they alone were "made in His image." They were creatures like all other forms of life, but they were more—the children of God. As their Creator, God gave mankind charge over the earth and all on it and commanded that people should "fill it up." He had confidence in His people and said, at the end of the creation-time, "It is good."

The Lord God really was a Father to Adam and Eve right from the start because He established and maintained a relationship with them in which He communicated—talked with them—in the garden. Do you remember the old Gospel hymn

> He walks with me and He talks with me
> And He tells me I am His own . . .?

58

It really belongs to Adam and Eve and the Genesis story. That's exactly what things were like at first. But the communication and the relationship broke down when Satan entered the picture tempting them to taste the fruit of the forbidden tree. "You will not die," he told them. "Your eyes will be opened . . . you will be like gods."

The pattern of Adam and Eve in the Garden holds for most of us when "our eyes are opened." We like to think that we lose our naivete, but we really lose our innocence and our purpose in life. We turn from the service of God and others to self-service and personal ambition.

Leslie Wayne, a reporter for the Philadelphia *Inquirer,* did a feature column last year about a woman—call her Donna—who changed careers and turned to a blackjack dealing-cocktail waitress "combination" from nursing. At 23 years of age she said, "I was just sick of illness. . . . I saw about the casinos (in Atlantic City, New Jersey) in the paper and I thought I'd try it. . . . Why not? You have to take a chance once in a while." After she had worked for some time in one of the plush gambling halls, she reported: "Basically, it's fun. . . . It's a good opportunity to be where the action is. Some people might say, 'I'm a secretary,' or 'I'm a receptionist.' But it's a little different to say, 'I'm a blackjack dealer.' . . . I looked at the people and I thought, 'I'm having more fun than the players.'" She expects to make $40,000 as a dealer— $500 in a bad week, over against her $200-something as a nurse. The "call of the casinos" was loud and clear—and she answered it! The world— not God's Word—set her agenda and guided her life.

How about us? It's often the old tragedy among the trees, isn't it? It's the human story we know so well, and we can't seem to do anything about it.

Temptation is just too much for us. We can't prevent ourselves from surrendering and becoming victims of sin—and right there we are separated from God and find ourselves living for ourselves alone. Right from the start of time we have misused our God-given freedom to obey or disobey God, to serve Him or serve ourselves. More often than not we say, "I just couldn't help myself. I just had to do it," and once again the special kind of relationship that has been renewed for us by Jesus Christ is strained to the breaking point—and we fall with Adam and Eve.

The Consequences of Sin

Adam and Eve got the shock of their lives when God found out what they had been up to when they encountered Satan and sin. They learned very quickly that they were not gods, and could not do anything they pleased on earth. They couldn't talk their way out of the dilemma they had created for themselves by their disobedience. They paid for their sin, as all people do sooner or later. God expelled them from the garden, which itself was something of an act of grace; they deserved extinction rather than expulsion. God's judgment included their earning of "bread" by the "sweat of their brow," and the unspoken suffering that people would know when they became hungry and had no bread. When anyone is hungry or starving it is finally a consequence of the garden-sin. And pain as a constant fact of life is inescapable.

The tragedy in the garden also brought about death. All people are marked for death, no matter who they are—rich or poor, young or old, intelligent or of limited mental powers, ambitious or lazy, healthy or sickly, white, red, yellow or black. Sooner or later everyone who is "born of woman" will die. There is no escape from the fatal consequences of sin. Life-support machines and systems are capable of sustaining "life" in sick or injured persons for almost unlimited amounts of time, but in the end death takes over. God's pronouncement was, "You are dust and unto dust you shall return." This has not been, and cannot be, circumvented. In the end we will all die.

While scientists predict that human beings will live over 100 years on the average during the next century, death cannot be destroyed by scientific means. One way or another, it will claim us all as its victims. Thus Horatio Bonar once spoke an eternal truth about the reality of death and the need to make the most of life while we have it:

> Make haste, O man! to live
> For thou so soon must die;
> Time hurries past thee like the breeze;
> How swift its moments fly.
> Make haste, O man! to live.

We do live longer since he penned those lines, but the truth is still the same, unto dust we shall return. Is there no way to get rid of this burden we bear as long as we live?

The Drama in the Desert

Since God spoke the word—death—to all of us, only He could lift the curse and restore us to life and eternal communion with Himself. He would do this through the woman's Seed, His own Son Jesus Christ. Out in the desert near the Dead Sea Christ spent 40 days in prayer and meditation after he was baptized in the Jordan River. Satan tempted Him in much the same way that Adam and Eve were tempted in the Garden of Eden, but Satan met his match with words that turn everything around to the way it was in the beginning: "Man shall not live by bread alone [or apples], but by every word that proceeds from the mouth of God" (Matt. 4:4). With these words Satan was defeated and put in his place, and what happened on the cross was confirmation of

God's victory in Christ. Christ did for people what they couldn't do for themselves in the garden or since the expulsion from the garden.

Death remains as the final enemy that all people have to face in their lives, but we have a new perspective on it now. It is a new beginning rather than an abrupt, final end. For death brings us closer to God and the fuller life in the kingdom that is to come. Death informs us that we are creatures whose lives must come to an end, but Christ's victory over Satan and sin removes the sting of death and assures us that we are and will be forever children of God. We are not returned to the garden, but we are restored to fellowship with our Father-God.

To live as the children of God is to live in the expectation that someday the fullness of that fellowship will be realized as one of the blessings of the resurrection. Only then will death be finally destroyed and life eternal become our reality. In the meantime we need not become morbid about the curse, "You are dust and unto dust you shall return." In the interim we have life and may live it to the fullest—for we are the children of God—once more and forever.

Here's where our baptism comes into the picture. Not only are we sealed through water, Word, and Spirit into a Father-child relationship with our God, but we know that we are baptized "in the name of the Son"—that His victory is really ours. Because in Holy Baptism our sins are forgiven and eternal life is promised to us, we live with the reality of "blessed assurance" in all our struggles, pain, and suffering, and we need fear nothing at all, including death—our worst and final enemy.

About a month and a half before he died, the much-loved pastor and professor Dr. Thomas Coates wrote a letter from Hong Kong to his friends in the United States. He thanked them for cards and greetings that had been sent to him during his illness, and he spoken openly about his losing battle with cancer: "When I heard the dread word on September 15, after a stunned moment I felt a calmness and peace ('the peace which passeth all understanding') that has remained with me and sustained me ever since." He continues: "Surely, there have been tears— but these have been tears of nostalgia for friends. But otherwise—I can look forward to the future only with joy and expectation."

He ended the letter on this note: "I must draw to a close, dear friends. I am reminded of a letter that my beloved mother wrote to me toward the end of her life. I was on a brief trip, and she wrote: 'I can hardly wait!' And so I can say: 'I can hardly wait!'" With Dr. Coates we know that through Christ and in Holy Baptism all is really well in our world and for us. As it was at the beginning, we are the children of God—and so it will be forever. Our loving Father has seen to this! Amen.

Second Sunday in Lent

New Life for Children of God

Genesis 7:1-5, 11-12, 17-23

A few years ago, a newspaper in Hawaii printed a feature article with the headline, "New Life for the Chosen Few." Beneath the caption was the photo of a man seated on the deck of a 44-foot sailing craft. His name was Jan Newhouse. The accompanying story related his fears that human beings are destroying the earth and themselves by polluting the earth, using up its resources, and producing nuclear energy that threatens all life on earth. The writer went on to say that Jan Newhouse believes that the present course toward self-destruction will be irreversible in about 10 years. He reached that conclusion by reading every book and article available on the ecological crisis—not as an ordinary, frightened person might do, but as a scientist. Dr. Jan Newhouse teaches science at the University of Hawaii.

Newhouse simply did not talk or write about his fear that the earth, as we know it, might come to an end; he went into action. He discovered 18 small atolls in the South Pacific that "will support life," and he made plans to organize expeditions of carefully chosen individuals who would be transported to these small coral islands and their "secret meadows" in the hope of preserving life on the earth. He proceeded to purchase a sailboat with an auxiliary engine and, at the time of the article, was in the process of selecting volunteers for the experiment that could mean "new life for the chosen few." Those selected would be people with special intellectual, physical, and emotional gifts, and their society will be, if Newhouse succeeds in his venture, an exclusive elitist group. He believes that such people—and nothing was said about goodness or morality—are the best chance that humanity has to survive the threat of total destruction of all life on earth. He is a new Noah, and he might very well have named his boat the "Ark II."

God's Wrath, Judgment, and the Flood

Ten centuries or more, according to Genesis, after Adam and Eve were expelled from the Garden of Eden, God lost His patience with humanity. Sin covered the earth like a plague of locusts and God decided to do something about it. Once more He would return to the Creation—turn time backward by reducing the population of the earth to one family—Noah and his children. Only this good man and seven other persons on earth were worth saving! Even the animals, birds, and reptiles had to die in order to erase the scourge of sin and rebellion from the earth. Eight people and a multitude of animals were the "chosen few" who had been selected by God for survival. God's wrath and judgment were tempered by His love and mercy—and the "chosen few" were spared from the flood that covered the entire earth.

God chose Noah because he was close to the kind of persons God created in the beginning. Noah had four important qualities that commended him to God: First, he lived justly with his friends and neighbors—people found no fault with him; second, he "walked with God," (Gen. 6:9), and that was one of the things that Adam and Eve did in the garden before they disobeyed and were expelled; third, he obeyed God, and fourth, he trusted in the Word of God. Clearly, in the Old and New Testaments Noah is depicted as a man of faith who is living out his life in relationship with the Lord his God. As the "chosen one" of the Lord, Noah was put in charge of the entire operation which God planned to give His children a new start in life.

Today God still has His chosen few blessed with faith in Jesus Christ and destined for eternal glory with Christ. And we are included. "Whoever believes in Him [Jesus] shall not perish but have everlasting life." "Whoever lives and believes in Me," says Jesus, "shall never die" (John 11:26).

Noah believed God when He said: "I have determined to make an end of all flesh; for the earth is filled with violence through them; behold I will destroy them with the earth. Make yourself an ark of gopher wood . . . cover it inside and out with pitch. . . . For behold, I will bring a flood of waters upon the earth, to destroy all flesh in which is the breath of life from under heaven; everything that is on the earth shall die. But I will establish my covenant with you, and you shall come into the ark, you, your sons, your wife, and your sons' wives with you. From all living creatures, from all flesh, you shall bring two of every sort into the ark" (Gen. 6:13-14, 17-19). And so Noah got to work and built the ark and loaded it as God commanded him to do.

Imagine how people who admired and respected Noah must have reacted when, in answer to their questions, Noah told them what he was doing—and why. They must have thought that he had suddenly gone mad. Some of them must have roared with laughter at the thought of a flood that would cover the whole earth and eradicate every living creature from the face of it. God was remote, rather unreal to most people; the violence that marked their lives offered ample evidence of their unbelief and godlessness. But how could they have had any understanding of such a possibility? Nothing in their experience or in the history of humanity up to that point offered a clue that such a catastrophe might actually be possible. And when the Flood came as the water rose during those forty days and forty nights and there was nowhere, no way to escape the torrent, many of them must have shrieked, "If only we had listened, rather than laughed, when Noah told us why he was building that boat!" But it was too late for repentance, and the waters inundated the highest mountains so that everything—all flesh—perished in the flood. Only Noah and his family survived the deluge and its aftermath.

Times have changed since then, at least in one respect. We have been able to perceive the possibility of the destruction of all life on earth in this age. That's partly why Dr. Jan Newhouse's picture and story made headlines. He may have seemed a little odd to some persons, even too much of an alarmist and too realistic for the majority of us who want to hang on to our way of life at all cost. Countless other persons— philosophers, theologians, humanists, as well as scientists—have warned us all that we are well into the process of destroying the earth and, possibly, all life.

Sixteen years after she died, Rachel Carson was honored for her pioneering efforts in alerting people to the reality of possible self-destruction. She merited the Presidential Medal of Freedom for her literary-scientific masterpieces that have made us aware of the danger that threatens all life. She dedicated the best known of her works, *Silent Spring,* to Albert Schweitzer who was one of the first persons to comprehend our predicament. He had said: "Man has lost the capacity to foresee and to forestall. He will end by destroying the earth." In the 16 years since her death, we have become conscious of the problems we have created by attempting to control nature through the use of chemical pesticides. And while nuclear war still poses a terrible threat to all life on earth, it is increasingly obvious that we are threatening to destroy life by our misuse of the good earth and its resources.

What the Flood Accomplished

After being cooped up in the ark for most of a year, Noah and his family were finally able to disembark, release all of the animals that had been with them, and begin their rehabilitation to life on solid ground again. The first thing that was done was the erection of an altar so that thanks and praise might be offered to God for delivering them from the flood. They knew that they were the only eight people on earth who had survived the deluge and the flood that followed. God had kept the ark afloat, had enabled them to survive the wind and the waves—and the utter boredom of being shut up aboard that vessel for such an extended period of time. They fell down and worshiped their Deliverer, and no one has had better reason to bless God than they did.

The Lord God accepted the "fragrance" of their sacrifice and made a promise to the eight persons and their descendants: "Never again will I curse the earth because of man, because his heart contrives evil from his infancy. I will never again destroy every living creature as I have done. While the earth remains, seedtime and harvest, cold and heat, summer and winter, day and night shall not cease" (Gen. 8:21-22). With that God reiterated what had been said to humanity at the creation: Noah and his family were to take charge of the earth and everything on it and fill it up with people. Then God said, "This is the sign of the covenant which I make between Me and you and every living creature with you for all future generations: I set my bow in the clouds, and it shall be a sign of the covenant between Me and the earth" (Gen. 9:12-13). The rainbow is the sign of new life and a renewal of the relationship that existed at creation between God and His children. It is the symbol of forgiveness of the righteous God to His people.

The flood came as God's judgment upon sinful and disobedient creatures who had no appreciation of life or the God who gave it to them. The torrents of rain and the flood of water washed the earth clean of hatred, enmity, jealousy, and pride, as well as their fruits—dissension in families, murder among friends and relatives, and war between nations that should be friends. The ancient emotions and attitudes that smashed relationships between persons and between people and God suffered the sailor's death of drowning. That was, indeed, a radical way to cleanse the earth of sin by literally causing most of the people on earth to die by suffocation. But not only were eight persons saved from inundation and death, the earth itself was renewed by the flood so that it would be habitable again and support growth and the expansion of life. God's condemnation led to the cleansing of the earth and new life for "the chosen few" and all of their offspring.

The Flood and Our Baptism

Martin Luther, possibly because he was an Old Testament professor who also discovered what the New Testament had to say about God and His people, helps us to understand the connection between our lives and the flood in Holy Baptism. Among his earliest efforts to revise the liturgies of the church we find an "Order for Baptism" first prepared in 1523 and "newly revised" just three years later. Both orders contain a "Flood prayer"; it is abbreviated in the 1526 edition, but both begin the same way:

"Almighty, eternal God, who according to Thy righteous judgment didst condemn the unbelieving world through the flood and in Thy great mercy didst preserve believing Noah and his family, and who didst drown hardhearted Pharoah with all his host in the Red Sea and didst lead Thy people Israel through the same on dry ground, thereby prefiguring this bath of Thy baptism, and who through the baptism of Thy dear Child, our Lord Jesus Christ, has consecrated and set apart the Jordan and all water as a salutary flood and a rich and full washing away of sins: We pray through the same Thy groundless mercy that Thou wilt graciously behold this [person] and bless him with true faith in the Spirit so that by means of this saving flood all that has been born in him from Adam and which he himself has added thereto may be drowned in him and engulfed, and that he may be sundered from the number of the unbelieving, preserved dry and secure in the holy ark of Christendom, serve Thy name at all times fervent in spirit and joyful in hope, so that with all believers he may be made worthy to attain eternal life according to Thy promise; through Jesus Christ our Lord. Amen."

That was what Luther affirmed when he said, "I am baptized!" He understood that through Baptism he had joined the "company of eight"—the few who had received new life through the flood. Christ's baptism at the Jordan and then on the cross made it possible for Luther and for us.

> There is a fountain filled with blood
> Drawn from Immanuel's veins;
> And sinners plunged beneath that flood
> Lose all their guilty stains.

Those benefits become ours in our baptism. We, too, have been cleansed of our sin through a "little flood" and are restored among the chosen to whom new life has been given by God. Our business is to respond in thanksgiving, prayer, and sacrifice as we attempt to live out the model Noah patterned and which Christ completely exemplified: to live justly with people, to "walk" with God, to obey the commands of our God, and to trust His Word. The flood and Baptism ought to converge in our observance of Lent and Easter, because when they do, they mean "new life" for the chosen, the children of God. Amen.

Third Sunday in Lent

God Relents When His People Repent

Jonah 3:1-10

Nineveh must have been a kind of "sin city." Why else would God have threatened it with destruction? Conditions were so bad in the great city that God did an amazing thing: He chose Jonah and charged him with the business of going to Nineveh to preach to the people, warning them of impending disasters and calling on them to repent and believe in God. What is even more amazing is that they listened to Jonah when he preached; they took his message seriously, and they repented of their sin by fasting and wearing sackcloth and ashes. That sort of thing doesn't happen very often—either in great cities or in small towns or villages. It is almost incredible that an entire city would confess its wickedness in this manner and receive forgiveness from God. God does relent and withhold punishment when people repent of their sins and evil doings.

On rare occasions as a national tragedy, a widespread catastrophe, or a threat of substantial proportions such signs of repentance are in evidence. It takes a threat to people's existence, usually, to bring forth the signs—an impending natural phenomenon which can't be controlled and sometimes not even understood. When a total eclipse of the sun recently threw a 900-mile-wide shadow across Africa and Asia, animals as well as people were confused and frightened—some almost to death. In Kenya posters were distributed in advance to quiet fears that the eclipse would signal the end of the world for some tribesmen, but a Kenyan astrologer warned pregnant women that "they would lose their children if they ventured outdoors during the eclipse." There were reports that "some tribes in Zaire's equatorial jungles barricaded themselves in their huts to ward off evil spirits."

The most bizarre reaction to the eclipse occurred in Konarek, in eastern India, where "thousands gathered to worship and dispel the evil influences of the eclipse." And "others chanted and buried themselves up to their necks in cow dung in prayers against what they believed were influences of the eclipse" (UPI). Words—especially in the form of preaching—seldom have that kind of an impact upon people, particularly when they've been said so many times before and nothing seems to have happened. But in Nineveh even the king listened, took them seriously, and led the ceremonies of repentance that he called for by putting on sackcloth and sitting in ashes himself.

A call to repentance is most appropriate in view of the forces of destructive nature running amuck in our world. Certainly all people need to reflect seriously on the quality of their lives and "sort out" through reflection, repentance, and positive action those elements which threaten moral decay and the actual destruction of society and its institutions. But this message is intended for people who are observing Lent as a time of serious self-examination and genuine repentance, particularly in the light of the meaning of Baptism. We are not the people of Nineveh; we are the forgiven children of God, who have received God's mercy and His promise of life in Holy Baptism. And in Baptism and repentance we find new meaning for our lives.

God Loves All the People of the World

One of the indisputable facts about our God is that He loves all of His creation and particularly all the people in His creation. And He does not desire that anyone should come to destruction. This kind of love is often lacking in people-to-people relationships. We don't have to be very perceptive to realize that there is a little bit of the "spirit of Cain" in all of us. A pastor tells about a visit he made to Philadelphia, the City of Brotherly Love, for orientation to the inner-city parish system that exists there. He and the system supervisor were on their way to lunch. They had to stop at a street corner and wait for the traffic light to change before they could cross the street. Suddenly their attention was caught by two men who ran up the street directly across from where they were standing; one was obviously chasing the other. He caught up with the man on the opposite corner and right before their eyes pulled out a gun, fired several shots point blank into the other man's chest, and stood over him after he fell. A police squad car drove up to the scene, but the officers didn't have to chase the gunman; he threw down his gun, then began to jump up and down where he was, almost chanting, "I killed him! I killed him at last! I killed that no good so and so!" One of the differences between God and ourselves is that, as the Nineveh story shows, God does not want to destroy *any* of His children. Even the worst of sinners is given an opportunity to repent and live.

To those who repent of their sins and return to Him, God offers and gives forgiveness for their sins no matter how grievous they may be. Just as He sent Jonah to Nineveh, He sent Jesus—and His forerunner, John the Baptist—to call us back from our evil ways in true repentance and faith, ere the day of grace be ended. Christ offers pardon and reconciliation with the Father when we deserve nothing but God's wrath and displeasure. From our standpoint God's forgiveness is really "too good" for us; we don't, we can't, deserve it. But He freely offers love and forgiveness to the world and each of us through the cross of Christ. When Jesus gave His life at Calvary, that made it possible for all people to *see* God's love and to enjoy the forgiveness Christ offers. Remember that Christ said, "And I, when I am lifted up from the earth, will draw all men to Myself" (John 12:32). The sight of the crucified Christ ought to smash us to our knees with a cry on our lips, "God, be merciful to me, a sinner!"

Those who really repent and know themselves to be forgiven do an abrupt "about face" in their lives, allowing the Spirit of God to take over and direct their actions and relationships with other people. Now and then this phenomenon surfaces in God's children before the watching world; "they know we are Christian by our love" as we "forgive those who have sinned against us" because we know that God has forgiven us. A few years ago Don Ehrlichmann, a high school teacher who had devoted his life to young people, was taking his youngest son to work. As was his habit, he picked up three hitchhikers—one of whom almost immediately drew a gun. He smashed the car into a tree and yelled, "Jump!" to his son; both leaped from the car and ran, but the youth with the gun followed the teacher and fired. Erlichmann died almost instantly; the three young men fled. Just three days later, Jim Klobuchar, columnist for the Minneapolis *Star*, published a letter sent him by Erlichmann's widow. It read, in part:

During the past three days my grief and desolation have been eased and comforted . . . by the love and faith of so many wonderful friends and relatives. But in the midst of all of this, and especially in the quiet moments, my thoughts keep turning to you three. . . . I wonder to whom you are turning for comfort, strength and reassurance. . . . I suppose I will never know what motivated your actions that night, but if the shots were fired out of sheer panic, my heart aches for you and I wish there were only some way I could help you in what you are suffering now. If hate made you pull the trigger, I can only pray that you can come to know the love of God that fills the heart and leaves no room for hate. If you were under the influence of drugs, please, for my sake and your own, don't waste your lives, too. Get help and rid yourselves of that stuff. Please, if you see this, find a church some place where you can be alone; then read this again. *Know that God forgives you and that my family and I forgive you* [italics, mine]; then go out and make something worthwhile out of the rest of your lives. God bless and keep you.

That kind of an offer was made to Nineveh—and that is exactly what

God intends for us in Jesus Christ, our Lord. God relents when His people repent—and return to Him.

The Cross Calls All People to Repentance

The cross and the death of Jesus Christ add a new dimension to the Old Testament story of His mercy upon a city that deserved to be destroyed, even leveled to the ground. We know that God was in that awful event "reconciling the world to Himself." God was there, not as a bystander observing the proceedings or even as the powerful Holy Spirit that supported the Savior in His sufferings. The cross is the announcement that God has taken our sins upon Himself in Jesus Christ. The cross of Christ calls us to repentance, not simply to watch the proceedings or do some acts of devotion. It really was for us that He hung there. We need to realize during Lent that He didn't deserve death. He was totally innocent and completely obedient to the Father. If ever a human *deserved* the Father's love and blessing, Jesus Christ was that person. But despite His righteousness He received what we deserved; and that ought to make us stop and think, and especially pray, "Lord, have mercy!"

The righteousness of Christ strips away all of our defenses. Perhaps when we compare conditions in our cities and land with Nineveh, we might comprehend that we are no better than they were—we might be worse because we claim to "know" Jesus Christ as our Lord. But it is too easy to compare ourselves and our righteousness with people we see around us, live with, work with. We often see ourselves in comparison with others as good people. We don't deliberately hurt other people, and we don't eliminate our enemies by murdering them. We try to do God's will, and we go to church regularly, thank Him for our blessings, and attempt to serve Him. What do we have to repent about? When, as we do especially in the season of Lent, we examine ourselves in the light of the cross, we know that only Christ was sinless and that He alone of all people lived out His life perfectly within the Father-Child relationship established long ago. Christ suffered the fate that we disobedient and self-willed creatures have earned, while we benefit now and eternally by His sacrifice on our behalf at the cross.

Without the cross of Christ and Lent's call to repentance, we are in danger of missing the root-problem in our relationship with God the Father. The true picture is not always what it seems to be. A Swedish theologian once compared our lives to a little lake in his hometown. It was in a beautiful setting, almost idyllic. Trees surrounded it and framed the blue waters with green leaves in the summer. People boated on it, even swam in the rather clean-looking water; there was a nice beach on one end of it. But he discovered, gradually, what the rest of the lake bottom was like. Leaves had accumulated and had rotted into a deep layer of "muck"—and people had thrown all sorts of refuse into it—bottles, cans, tires, among other things. It appeared to be such a lovely lake—on the surface—but the farther you went below the surface the worse its condition got. And the theologian insists that that lake became a picture of our spiritual condition; we are in danger of seeing those things on the surface of life—and we don't come off too badly on that level. But the sinless death of Jesus Christ forces us to look into the very depths of our hearts and souls to see "if there is any sin in us," and you and I know that one glance is enough to tell us what our real condition is. We know that only Christ is righteous in Himself; the rest of us are in a predicament, and only He can get us out of it.

Baptism—Our Daily "Dip"

John Leonard of the New York *Times* once described our way of life as one made up of "disposable relationships: No promises required." He believes that ours is an era of temporary relationships that result from a lack of commitment to each other. Therefore we conclude our relationships when we wish for any reason or no reason at all. *We* have declared that we can do no wrong when actually we know better. Our relationship with God is, if not entirely "disposable," *intermittent*, at best. We know that we can't quite get along without Him, so we put Him "on the back burner" in the hope that He will be there when we really need Him—as we all do in the face of physical death—for support and deliverance. Deep down, if we allow His Word and Spirit to strip away our pretensions and see ourselves as we really are—we know that our relationship with God is not disposable. Lent reminds us of that!

And the cross of Christ reminds us that we are baptized! God wants us as His forgiven children, and He has in our baptism sealed us into that Father-child relationship. When, as the water was poured, the pastor said, "I baptize you in the name of the Father, and of the Son, and of the Holy Spirit," we were given a name as a child of God and entered into a permanent relationship. God never withdraws from His part in that covenant between the Father and His children, but in the sinful spirit of the world we strain the baptismal connection and by our sin break the bond that binds us to God. Repentance and reconciliation between the Father and us are bound up with our baptism. Lent reminds us of that, too.

We turn away from God and sin every day that we are alive; that's why we need in spirit a "daily dip" in the font—to remind us that we are God's children forever, to convict us of our sin and bring us to the "little death" of the font through Baptism, and to wash us clean and renew us so that we may go forth to life in the knowledge that despite all we have been and done we are children of God. Baptism is the sign of an indispensable relationship, but it needs to be renewed by "daily dying and rising" with Christ through repentance and faith. We need a baptismal bath "in the name of the Father, and of the Son, and of the Holy Spirit" every day. Remember the rhythm of our relationship with God through Baptism! Baptism is administered only one time, but it has to be renewed over and over again as long as we live. In reality it is not simply a one-time experience that happened in our past; it is renewed whenever we say in repentance, "I renounce the devil and all his works and all his ways," and cling to Christ in faith.

We die—and are buried with Christ—when we make or "say" the sign of the cross in remembrance and renewal of our Baptism. Lent calls us to the cross and places us before the font and tells us to repent of our sin and separation from God and to plunge into the "death" of those waters. The cross, more positively than Jonah's sermon in Nineveh, reassures and encourages us: God relents and gives forgiveness and new life when His people repent. He restores us as children of God for eternity. Amen.

From Fast to Feast

Isaiah 55:1-11

Lent is the season in which we move through a fast to a feast. This happens as we keep the discipline of Lent—prayer, self-sacrifice, and almsgiving—in the 6½-week period, especially if our Lenten observances furnish us with new insight into the character of the Lord our God. In her book *Shikasta: Canepus in Argos-Archives,* Doris Lessing reminds us that God is not always what we would like Him to be: "It is our habit to dismiss the Old Testament altogether, because Jehovah, or Jahve, does not act like a social worker." The cross corrects our perspective of God by confronting us with the mystery of God's full-orbed love. He is not—in the Old Testament *or* the New Testament—exactly what we would like Him to be, nor does He do things the way we think they ought to be done. "My ways are not your ways," says the Lord, and again, "My thoughts are not your thoughts."

The fate of Jesus Christ forces us to contemplate what God is really like. The Creator of heaven and earth should have been able to find another way of accomplishing what He intended, another method of demonstrating His love for humanity than the route He chose—Calvary. If God is all-knowing, as well as all-powerful, He ought to have been able to find an alternative to the sacrificial death of Christ on the cross. It is in the death-event of Golgotha that God separates Himself from all the other gods that people have perceived, or created—and worshiped. And Lent not only beckons us to comprehend what God did in Jesus' death, but it is the time when we prepare to participate in the Easter event.

The Fast—an Invitation

It is traditional to view Lent as the invitation to a fast; Lent is an invitation in itself—to a feast. The fast is never complete by itself; it cannot exist apart from the feast and the new life in Jesus Christ. The discipline of Lent prepares us to celebrate the victory feast, partly because it reminds us what it cost God to accomplish our salvation. He

73

did what He set out to do in Jesus Christ. In Jesus Christ's death and resurrection God made us acceptable to Himself by freely forgiving our sins. When we begin to penetrate this mystery, we are restored to fellowship with the Father, and new life throbs through our beings.

Now and then this mystery surfaces in human relationships. Two couples were having marital difficulties. In one family, the wife had been unfaithful to her husband; in the other, it was the husband who had violated the marriage vows. Both couples attempted to reconcile their differences through marital counseling, but the first couple was divorced, the second stayed together. The offended husband could not bring himself to forgive his wife, but the wounded wife, whose mate had deliberately tried to hurt her by flaunting his affair to her, was able to forgive him. And with them it is like Ann Landers said in one of her columns: if the wife is able to forgive—and the husband accepts her love and forgiveness—their marriage may become better than it was before. Forgiveness unleashes the power of God's love in human relationships as well as in divine-human encounters. As the forgiving wife replied when asked how she could continue to live with her husband and forgive him, "I love him very much." And when she heard that the first couple had been divorced—and why—she remarked: "That's too bad. He needs to learn to forgive. I could teach him forgiveness. . . . To keep hate locked up inside you makes you sick. Forgiveness restores you to health—and happiness, too."

That lesson is learned at the cross of Jesus Christ—and it is relearned during the fast of Lent. We keep Lent so that we might know that we are forgiven; God has removed our sins from us by His love and goodness. That's why we culminate the fast with a feast! Remembering and reliving God's love and mercy in the events of Jesus' passion, perfect obedience, and absolute trust in the face of death opens us up to rebirth and new life through the remission of our sins. God has pardoned each one of us—the cross tells us this—so we accept the invitation to the feast with joy and anticipation—right in the middle of the fast.

Accepting God's Invitation

The discipline and devotions of Lent are the means whereby we accept, as well as probe, the Bible for understanding and comprehension of the mystery of the cross, the invitation to the feast. Lent is the season of the Kyrie, "Lord, have mercy." The cross rips the blinders from the eyes of our souls so that we may pray, "We have sinned against You in thought, word, and deed, by what we have done and what we have left undone." The cross gives confidence to our confession so that we might add, "Make us fit for Your presence, Lord." A true and right confession is essential to keeping the Lenten fast.

But Lent is also the time when we affirm our love for God and assert our eternal gratitude to Father and Son for what has been accomplished for, and offered to, us. Savonarola puts words into our mouths with his hymn:

> Jesus, may our hearts be burning
> With more fervent love for Thee!
> May our eyes be ever turning
> To Thy Cross of agony
> Till in glory, parted never
> From the blessed Savior's side,
> Graven in our hearts forever,
> Dwell the cross, the Crucified!

And if our hearts "burn" with "more fervent love" for Christ, that love ought to be given expression every day of the 40-day fast.

"Tell them now you love them" is the title of a moving column written by Darrell Sifford shortly after the death of his father. It is a tribute to his father—almost an eulogy—but also an expression of his love for his father. Sifford says that he wrote to his parents at least twice a week for the five years before his father died; he sent them every column that he published. He tells that he once wrote a column about his father, and how when he went home they would sit on the floor and "drill into the core of life."

Sifford writes: "I asked what it felt like when the only son moved 1,000 miles from home, when the grandchildren were rarely seen, when the only son separated and divorced and wrote a letter asking for understanding and acceptance, when the only son and the father disagreed on what religion was or ought to be and its relevance in daily living." He also asked his father about "his perception of what it would be like to die," and how "his answer was that he feared death until he came to understand that death was not the end but the beginning." His father had said, "When a man believes, when a man does his best to get right with God, with his fellowman, with himself—well, death is nothing to be afraid of." He said that his father told him how much he loved him because "love needs to be spoken."

"Pop and I didn't leave anything unsaid," writes Darrell Sifford, and that's why one of the last things he said to his father was, "You and Mom are responsible for making possible everything I have achieved in life. There is no way I can ever thank you enough for what you have done for me." That's in sharp contrast to those who blame their parents for their fate and failures in life, isn't it? Sifford's father replied, "Only a father can know how good it feels to hear a son say that." Our devotions, especially in Lent, ought to have that quality about them, "Father, we thank Thee for . . ."

The fact of the Father's forgiveness puts the words of love and devotion for God into our hearts and upon our lips. And God's heart is warmed by our expressions of love and gratitude for Him. He wants to hear us say, "I love you, Lord, with all my heart and soul and strength and mind," and then to see the lives we live bear this love out in the concern, compassion, and care we show for the people of the world.

Worship and work combine in our lives—and especially in Lent—to give shape to a liturgy that is pleasing and acceptable to God. Gerard Sloyan once wrote: "The liturgy is not in itself Christian life. It is the sign of that life." Our liturgy of worship and work are testimony to God's love and forgiveness in our lives, not merely in our mouths or on our tongues. Father Sloyan adds: "Real life is about things like children who come to school without breakfast, about Negro high schools which have one all-purpose lab with one electrical outlet and one Bunsen burner. It is about the thousands who confess . . . and the millions who don't and the . . . clergy everywhere who are confused and demoralized over the counsel they must give them. Real life has to do with signs all over the world." We think of hunger, poverty, injustice, hatred, disease. Lent reminds us that the poet was right:

> And if I said, "I love Thee, Lord,"
> He would not heed my spoken word,
> Because my daily life would tell
> If verily I loved Him well.

The acceptance of God's forgiving love and its expressions in words of adoration and works of mercy are the signs that we are His children.

Water and Our Baptism

When Isaiah issued his invitation on behalf of God, "Come to the waters," he was thinking of God's everlasting mercy, not Christian baptism. But Lent reminds us that God first gave each of us the sign of His love and forgiveness in our baptism. And should we find ourselves among the "thirsty" during Lent and its fast, the feast before us promises, as we prepare to celebrate Jesus' death, resurrection, and return at the end of time, to renew that gift of God's grace poured out upon most of us when we were infants. That's really what the Easter Eucharist does too; it restores our souls through the forgiveness of sins given us first in Holy Baptism—at the beginning of our life as children of God. Preparing for and keeping the feast is what the Lenten fast is all about. Amen.

The Incredible Sacrifice

Genesis 22:1-18

Early in 1972 Joseph Kramer, a Jew who had escaped from Latvia during the Nazi invasion, could not control his emotions when a Torah scroll was dedicated in a Tel Aviv synagog in memory of his 16-month-old son who died in that invasion. He sobbed openly for a child who had died almost three decades before that day—and with good reason. Joseph Kramer had constructed a bunker beneath his home in Latvia and, on the night the Nazis entered their town, he, his wife, and son shared that hiding place with 45 of their neighbors. His son, David, was frightened by the noise of the approaching soldiers and began to cry. Efforts to calm him failed; he became hysterical—and as his wife and neighbors looked on, Joseph Kramer did the only thing he could think of—he placed his hand across the nose and mouth of his son—and smothered him. And despite the knowledge that his action was an act of deliverance for those Jews—all escaped and some were present that day in Tel Aviv, the memory of that awful deed—and its terrible agony—was overwhelming. He could not be comforted.

Unbelievable Obedience

The acccount of God's demand that Abraham take his son, his only child, to the land of Moriah and offer him as a sacrifice to God shocks the minds of people today. Without question, Abraham did as the Lord instructed him to do—took his son, Isaac, two servants, wood, fire, knife, and a donkey and set off on a three-day journey. When they reached the place, the servants were told to wait and mind the donkey while Abraham took Isaac to sacrifice him according to the custom by which animals were slaughtered. He did not hesitate for a moment; he built the altar, stacked firewood, tied up Isaac, and raised his knife to kill his son, just as God had directed him to do. But at the last moment God intervened through an angelic messenger, "Abraham, Abraham! . . . . Do not lay your hand on the lad or do anything to him, for now I know that you fear God, seeing you have not withheld your son, your only son from Me" (Gen. 22:11-12). Abraham dropped his knife, saw a ram caught by its horns in a bush, and he went and took the sacrifice that God had provided and made a burnt offering *of the ram* to God.

When the Abraham-Isaac story is held up to the Kramer story, it seems that most of the emotion has been drained from it. When Isaac asks that bothersome question of his father, "But where is the lamb for the burnt offering," Abraham's answer expresses deep faith but little emotion: "My son, God Himself will provide the lamb for the burnt offering." But God didn't intervene until Isaac had been tied up and placed on the firewood and the knife raised to kill him. How could he have looked at his son? He must have had to avoid the look in Isaac's eyes, because he suddenly realized, as he lay there, that he was to be the sacrificial lamb. That scene—his son lying on the wood and the altar and his standing there, upraised knife in hand—must have been burned into his memory for the rest of his life. He had almost slain and sacrificed his son, bone of his bone, and flesh of his flesh, in the belief that God wanted him to do this "for His sake." God's children love their children and sacrifice for them rather than sacrificing them in the name of God. People do their best to love their children as they know that their Father loves them. Only religious fanatics or madmen are likely to take the lives of their children, declaring, "God told me to do it." Rational people with faith don't even consider doing such things.

The sudden and tragic death of a loved one, particularly an only child, seems almost to be the ultimate test of our faith. The telephone rang in a pastor's home and a voice on the other end delivered terrible news: "Jeff is dead. He was killed by a truck the day after Thanksgiving." Just about a year before that call, the phone had rung and Jeff's grandfather announced, "Sandy is going to die." Sandy was Jeff's 32-year-old mother; she had been waging a 3½ year battle with cancer but now cancer was gaining the upper hand. The doctors, her father said, had given her about three months to live. She died, almost on schedule, at the beginning of the same year in which her son was so tragically killed. After her death her mother had said, "Jeff, plus wonderful memories, is all we have left of Sandy now." Her mother and father both wondered why God had allowed their daughter to die; she was a fine young woman, a loving daughter, wife, and mother. She was useful to others, participating actively in a program to encourage other cancer victims who had to endure cancer surgery like hers and the pain and agony that go with it. Now their grandson, too, was dead; how must they have felt about God the day after Thanksgiving when their telephone rang? They must have asked that familiar question, "What kind of a God do we have?"

Abraham might have been a "shattered" man, if he had gone

through with the sacrifice of Isaac. He might even have turned away from God; at least, his faith would have been more severely tested than it was when he set off for Moriah with Isaac and the servants. Fortunately, God stopped the descent of the blade at the last moment. Suddenly, we see what God is really like; He demands that we trust and obey Him, but He desires the death of none of His people, especially not the death of little children.

God's Amazing Love

God is the central character in the Abraham-Isaac story in the Bible, and God's love is clearly revealed in this dramatic tale. Somehow or other, God's love for His creatures was evident to Abraham in that terrible time of testing, and God's love enabled him to tell Isaac, "God Himself will provide the sacrifice." From our perspective, we see the foreshadowing of Jesus' sacrifice on the cross—His passion and death. John saw this and put it boldly in his familiar, "God so loved the world that He gave His only begotten Son" statement; clearly, God Himself has provided the only sacrifice that will do to gain us forgiveness of our sins, reconciliation with Himself, and life in the age to come. God's love in offering His only Son as our Sacrifice is utterly amazing. He "paid the price" in Christ for us all:

> There was no other good enough
> to pay the price of sin;
> He only could unlock the gate of heaven
> and let us in.

God knew quite well what He was doing on Calvary, and Jesus knew exactly what was happening, and why. That's part of the difference between the Abraham-Isaac story and the God-Christ drama at the cross. Jesus didn't ask His Father, "Where is the lamb for the sacrifice?" He knew that He was the sacrificial Lamb and that His heavenly Father was demanding that He should lay down His life. When He took Peter, James, and John into the garden with Him, He said, "My soul is very sorrowful, even to death; remain here, and watch" (Mark 14:34). Mark continues, "And going a little farther He fell on the ground and prayed that, if it were possible, this hour might pass from Him. And He said, 'Abba, Father, all things are possible to Thee; remove this cup from Me; yet not what I will, but what Thou wilt'" (Mark 14:35-36). Luke adds that an angel appeared to Him, as with Abraham, not to deter Him or rescue Him from death, but to strengthen Him, adding: "Being in an agony He prayed more earnestly, and His sweat became like great drops of blood falling down upon the ground" (22:44). And our Lord was able to respond affirmatively to His Father's will, "Not My will but Thine be done." Father and Son were united in love—and the Lord could go to His death with "No one takes [My life] from Me, but I lay it down of My own accord" (John 10:18).

Few of us love each other—even close relatives—enough to suffer pain and risk death to "deliver" others from the threat of death.

A father once took his son to a Christmas Eve worship service. With "Joy to the World" and "Silent Night" ringing in their ears they left the church after the conclusion of the festive devotions. The young boy stepped off the curb ahead of his father; he didn't see the speeding car but his father did and pushed him out of the path of the auto only to be struck down—and killed instantly—himself. That boy will realize sometime, if not now, how much his father loved him; and he may also come to appreciate that God loves us the same way. Jesus was able to do what had to be done—to lay down His life so that all of God's children might be delivered from sin and death.

What kind of God demands His Son's life, especially when it has been lived out in perfect harmony and obedience to His will? Shouldn't a parent's love—and God's—be protective of child and children? Shouldn't it be self-sacrificing under all circumstances so as to preserve and improve the life of his/her children? There's more than a bit of the Father's love for His creatures in the man's act that saved his son's life at the cost of his own. God went even farther than that by sacrificing His own Son to save all of His own from separation and death. That was the costly way that God gave of Himself for all of us.

Abundant Grace

Baptism is a fitting sign of the Father's amazing love and His abundant grace toward His children, because it is connected to the cross of Jesus Christ. Jesus "became obedient unto death, even the death of the cross," but the Father was suffering with Him—"God was in Christ reconciling the world to Himself." We need to remember that when the waters closed over our heads in the "little death" of our baptism it was the cross of Jesus that separated the waters so that we could rise with Him. It took that death to win our release from the garden-curse, to set us free from sin and the power of Satan. Lent is the time that we need to remember that the blood of the crucified Christ drips into those waters and because of that fact—His sacrifice and the Father's—we are washed clean and made fit for the company of God. All that God can do for us as His children is contained in the knowledge that through Baptism and the sign of the cross we have been sealed into the Father's kingdom forever.

God said to Abraham, "Take your son, your only son Isaac . . . and offer him there as a burnt offering"; and Abraham almost did it. God stayed his hand. But on Golgotha, when Christ was in Isaac's predicament, God did not hold back the hands of those who drove the nails into Christ's hands and feet, nor did He quiet the tongues of those who threw taunts at Jesus: "If You are the Son of God, come down from the cross, and we will believe You." Nor did He stop the soldier who thrust the spear into the Savior's side to determine if He were really dead. The bloodless sacrifice of Isaac became a blood sacrifice, and the cross planted in the water of the font reminds us of that.

It's a long way from Jerusalem to Moriah and a longer distance to where we might be today. But whatever the distance, it has been bridged by God Himself, who provided the sacrificial ram at Moriah but gave His own Son at Jerusalem. In Baptism God the Father is telling us how much He loves us and that Jesus' death on the cross was for us. It took Jesus' sacrifice and the waters of Baptism to make us His children again. And God gives us the faith to believe that this is so and trust Him as our Father as long as we live. Amen.

Palm Sunday
(Sunday of the Passion)

The Passover and the Passion

Exodus 12:1-14, 29-34 (longer lesson—12; 14:10—15:1a)

Holy Week is the Christian Passover. It begins with the Palm Sunday procession that celebrates Christ's triumphal entry into Jerusalem where He is greeted and proclaimed as God's Promised One, the Deliverer. But the beginnings of this day, the Sunday of the Passion— and this Holy Week—come from another time, another place. The Passover of the Jews and the Christian Passover have common roots in a series of events that took place in Egypt over 3,000 years ago. There's a contemporary note in the basis of it—Moses' cry to Pharoah to relieve the plight of the people of God, whose status had been altered from invited guests in the time of Joseph to that of slaves whose lot was to make bricks and bake them in the hot Egyptian sun. "Let My people go!" rang out in that land of bondage and enforced labor. Adam had no idea of anything like this slavery when he and Eve were exiled from the garden and told to earn their bread "by the sweat of their brow!"

God's instructions to Moses spelled out all the details of Passover and the exodus that resulted from it: "On the tenth day of this month they shall take every man a lamb according to their fathers' houses, a lamb for a household; and if the household is too small for a lamb, then a man and his neighbor next to his house, shall take according to the number of persons, according to what each can eat you shall make your count for the lamb" (Ex. 12:3-4). The entire Passover procedure was explicitly outlined so that every person would know how to participate in it; no one would be able to say, "I didn't understand what I was supposed to do." And the people were made to understand most clearly that Passover and exodus were instituted by their God; what happened when the Jews were allowed by Pharoah to leave was comprehended by them as the work of God. The cry went up to Pharaoh throughout the land, "Let My people go!" but it was the God of the Hebrews who, through the 10 terrible plagues that culminated with the plague that took the life of the firstborn in every home in Egypt, was responsible for their release. Passover is not simply a revolutionary uprising by dissident slaves; it is God at work in human affairs demonstrating His Fatherly love for His children by setting them free from their slavery and leading them safely into the Promised Land.

It is a holy history: the nine plagues and the Passover plague, exodus, and pursuit by Pharaoh's army, the threat of death at the Red Sea and, through God, a path through the midst of the water, 40 years of hardship in the wilderness until at last the people of God reach and enter the Promised Land. God made certain that His chosen nation would never forget that experience: "This day shall be for you a memorial day, and you shall keep it as a feast to the Lord; throughout your generations you shall observe it as an ordinance forever" (Ex. 12:14). So it is—but Jesus Christ added a new dimension to it.

Holy Week—Remembrance and Reenactment

Holy Week is the time when we Christians recall and celebrate our deliverance from sin and death by the events that took place that week. The Sunday of the Passion is Palm Sunday for most of us—and many congregations have some type of special processional to relive Jesus' triumphant entry into Jerusalem. When we study the Scriptures and use our imaginations, we may almost "see" the procession coming into view as it left Bethphage—and we join it: we make our march into our churches to remember how it was when Jerusalem greeted the Christ, "Blessed is He that comes in the name of the Lord! Hosanna in the highest!" And we sing out:

> Ride on, ride on in majesty!
> In lowly pomp ride on to die.
> O Christ, Thy triumphs now begin
> O'er captive death and conquered sin.
> (Henry H. Milman, 1791-1868)

So we begin today the final stages of what turns out to be our Passover pilgrimage. Remembering what happened and acting it all out again brings the saving events done by God in Christ nearly 2,000 years ago into our time, our lives.

Trek to a Table

By joining the Palm Sunday procession and observing the day-by-day activities of our Passover, we make our way to the table that is central—and critical—to the observances of Holy Week. The Last Supper, as we so often call the Holy Communion instituted on Thursday of Holy Week, is a special "memory" and "reenactment" time for God's people in Christ.

After Jesus had given thanks and given the bread and the cup with the words "This is My body"; and "This is My blood shed for the forgiveness of sins," He told the disciples, as He reminds us this week: "Do this [as you eat and drink] in remembrance of Me" (Luke 22:19-20). The next day He would be dead, nailed to a criminal's cross; and ever after God's children, who believe Jesus Christ to be their Lord, sing, "Christ, our Passover, is sacrificed for us; let us celebrate the feast."

At the Table of the Lord in the middle of the celebrations of this Holy Week, we remember again what it was that God did—and how He did it. He dealt with our bondage to sin and death—and through Jesus' death and resurrection accomplished our Passover in Christ. One day He was very much alive; the next day He was dead, and right after the whole city of Jerusalem had shouted, "Blessed is He who comes in the name of the Lord." It was that way with Daphne du Maurier when her husband died. She had written about death many times in her novels, but all was different and final—and unexpected—when he suffered a heart attack: "It is only when death touches the writer in real life that he or she realizes the full impact of its meaning. The deathbed scene described so often becomes suddenly true. The shock is profound." Her reaction, after the initial "bewildered fits of weeping," she says, "was to blame myself. I could have done more during the last illness. I should have known, the last week, the last days, that his eyes followed me with greater intensity. I should never have left his side. How heartless, in retrospect, my last good-night, when he murmured to me, 'I can't sleep,' and I kissed him and said, 'You will, darling,' and went from the room." She describes how the next morning she went to his room, expecting the "usual smile," but, "he turned his face to me—and died by sudden coronary thrombosis. His eyes were open, but the spark had gone. What had been living was no more. This, then, was death." Jesus' last words on the cross were, "It is finished," and "Father, into Your hands I commit my spirit"—and He died. Who would have expected that week to end that way?

Jesus knew that His death was at hand and He almost seemed to orchestrate the end of His life that last week. The cleansing of the temple, His last teachings, the Supper, the Gethsemane prayer, betrayal, and arrest—and the trials—set the stage; but the frightened, disheartened, shame-faced followers of Jesus must have had difficulty realizing what was happening until His head fell forward and He collapsed—dead! That brings us, this week, to the table in the heart of it, where we are able to remember—and celebrate!—His death once more because we know the outcome—resurrection!—in advance. The reality of Christ's death makes the celebration of the resurrection dynamic, eventful, and exciting. "He is risen, indeed! Alleluia!"

Baptism and the Cross

There is a connection between the baptism of Jesus by John in the Jordan, when the Father stated, "This is my beloved Son," and the climax of Holy Week when the Father subjected His beloved Son to a second "baptism." It is important for us to see Jesus' baptism in terms of His death on the cross. When He said, after the Jordan experience and the death of John the Baptist, "I have a baptism to be baptized with, and how I am constrained until it is accomplished" (Luke 12:50), He was talking about His death at Calvary. His crucifixion, when He became the new Passover, was His "baptism." Jesus made it abundantly clear that He chose that second baptism; He might have avoided it. A few years ago there was a sequel to the well-known incident that occurred in Equador a quarter of a century ago when a group of Auca Indians murdered five American missionaries who hoped to preach the Gospel to them. Rachel Saint and a group of Aucas, including Gikita, the man who led the party that slaughtered the missionaries, toured several cities in America and told how she and Mrs. Betty Elliot returned to Equador and made contact with the savages. She said, "I explained to Gikita, many months later when there was confidence and understanding, that my brother had been in military service before flying mission planes down there. 'You were close; he easily could have killed you,' I told him more than once. 'My brother chose not to kill you, chose to die instead. You see, he loved you.'" Calvary was that kind of a choice; it was Jesus' baptism, and He submitted to it out of loving obedience for the Father and genuine love for those He knew to be His sisters and brothers.

What Jesus called His baptism announces to the world, "Christ, our Passover, is sacrificed for us!" So Paul wrote to the church at Corinth, adding: "For Jews demand signs and Greeks seek wisdom, but we preach Christ crucified, a stumbling block to Jews and folly to Gentiles, but to those who are called, both Jews and Greeks, Christ the power of God and the wisdom of God. For the foolishness of God is wiser than men, and the weakness of God is stronger than men" (1 Cor. 1:22-25).

The troublesome question put to us by Jesus Christ Himself: is "Are you able to drink the cup that I drink, or to be baptized with the baptism with which I am baptized?" (Mark 10:38). It is so easy to say with James and John, "We are able," when we are caught up in the spirit of Holy Week, and the emotion of the events gets to us. However, to think of baptism as literally dying with Christ by living in obedience to the will of God and sacrificing ourselves in love for others might send us scurrying away or retreating to what looks like the safety of the baptismal font. We had to be taken there, after all, we were babies when we were baptized and made children of God. We never intended to get so involved with self-sacrifice and a hazardous Christian life. But baptism is identifying with the bloody crucifixion of our Lord—and dying with Him in that "baptism" of His.

We remember and we dare to live those holy events, even to gather around the table where the whole story is spelled out once more. And like the Jews, who are taken back to the wilderness, the Red Sea, and Egypt, we discover that we are transported all the way back to the Passover-exodus experience in our lives—our baptism—and that right then and there God involved us with the mission, as well as the mercy, of Christ for the rest of our lives. Amen.

The Day of New Creation

Ezekiel 37:1-14 (read also Matthew 28:1-10)

Alleluia! Christ is risen. This is the best news the living can share with one another in memory of their departed loved ones fallen asleep in Jesus. It should be received and celebrated by all who are waiting for a reunion. But how can I, once dead, expect a new life with my loved ones? Was I not born with a sinful nature and so a child of God's wrath? Was I not dead spiritually? And have I not many, many times succumbed to the tricks of the devil and my own sinful flesh? Have the wages of sin been changed? No, the wages have not been changed. They have been paid by Jesus. Easter is God saying, "Let there be life": life with Christ here and life with God in bliss hereafter.

There's a church in Rome that not many tourists get to see, despite the fact that it is located on the famous Via Veneto (the foot of the street, actually), the Church of Santa Maria della Concezione. Natives call it the "Church of the Bones" because there are four rooms in the basement which comprise the cemetery of the Cappuchins, a Franciscan order, who occupy the church. Bones of hundreds of monks who have died and were buried here have been disinterred and are to be seen in each room; it has the look of a haunted house, or Halloween—piles of skulls, vertebrae arranged in geometrical designs, leg bones, arm bones, all disconnected. One room contains complete skeletons wired together and clothed in the Cappuchin habit, standing or seated on benches before several crosses planted in the earth over the graves of those monks who died most recently. The soil is from the Holy Land so as to bridge the Mediterranean Sea so that those who die in Christ might be buried in the soil that held Him for those three days. The motif in this valley of the "dry bones" is that of waiting expectantly for the resurrection. The dead as well as the living keep watch for the return of Christ and the day of new life—"And you shall know that I am the Lord, when I open your graves and raise you from your graves, O My people. And I will put My Spirit within you, and you will live" (Ezek. 37:13-14). The promise of that kind of a day, when the dead shall be raised up by

God, has been confirmed by the victory of Christ over death and the devil. "On the third day, He rose . . .," and that was indeed a mighty victory over all of His foes!

Death Could Not Dry Up Jesus' Bones

The tomb could not hold the Christ for very long. People had done their best to rid the earth of Him, but His death was a short-lived triumph for His enemies. He was back among the living again, and now more than ever was He a force to be reckoned with; God's firstborn became the first Person to conquer death. God raised up the One to whom He said, "You are My Son, My Beloved," at His baptism in the Jordan. And what He did for Jesus Christ, He offers to do, through Christ, for all people.

We know that Christ rose from the garden grave on the third day because His disciples and others saw Him on the day of resurrection and in the time between Easter and His ascension. Were there only a tale about an empty tomb to base our faith upon, Jesus' death and resurrection would not be the central action of God in the Gospels. But Easter celebrates the Resurrection, not as a concept or an idea or a human wish, but as a reality in the risen Lord. When His bones should have been in the process of disintegration, the women were confronted, according to Matthew, by the angel, who told them the unbelievable news. Matthew tells us Jesus met them and greeted them. They saw Him, heard Him, fell down, "took hold of His feet," and worshiped Him as Lord.

Easter is an encounter with the living Lord! Even so, we can't help but wonder at times about the Resurrection, despite all the evidence in the New Testament. Time, distance, and life in a scientifically oriented age and a secularly immersed society militate against the belief in an actual resurrection from the dead. "Dead" people often "live" again—resuscitated before the lack of oxygen causes irreparable brain damage, or attached to life-support machinery that keeps them "alive" in body, but often living a vegetable-like existence; but actual resurrection just doesn't happen. And so the "third-day experience" of the women and the disciples has to be taken on faith—and the word of the witnesses are only believable by the power of God's Holy Spirit. Therefore we may believe that in Jesus' conquest of the grave God speaks to the world once more, reassuring all who will listen and believe that He who made us in the beginning has redeemed us and saved us for all eternity.

Magic or Mystery?

The old claims: that Christ did not really die on the cross but collapsed after six hours, was placed in a tomb rather hurriedly, revived

88

and came forth, or that He actually did die but His body was stolen and hidden by His disciples, despite a sealed tomb and guards—find expression in every generation. Unbelievers have called the Resurrection "the greatest hoax in history." Such skeptics were recently joined by a once-famous evangelist who now calls himself an agnostic and has attempted to write a money-making novel about the discovery of the "bones of Jesus." Others contend that the purported resurrection of Jesus Christ was some kind of magic, even necromancy, or black magic; and so, if they think of it at all, wonder how it was done.

The resurrection of Jesus Christ is no illusion—some kind of magic—but it is a mystery, God's mysterious action in answer to Jesus' obedience and His "baptism unto death" on the cross. It doesn't have to be seen to be believed. It doesn't have to be explained to be accepted by people who hear the incredible story. Because it is a mystery, it may only be grasped by those who have been given that equally mysterious gift of God—faith—that comes through the Word, water, and the Holy Spirit—and is reaffirmed when the story is told today and the "bread is broken" at His table.

God's Mystery and Our Creation

The resurrection of Jesus Christ confronts us with the mystery of God's creation. We celebrate His power to sustain and renew what He made at the beginning of time—life and living creatures on this planet. Easter asserts that the God who created us and gave us life has the power to preserve that life by reversing the death process forever. Easter used to be—and ought to be today—a celebration of God's power to create and re-create; it is fitting that the risen Lord was first encountered in a garden because He is the new Adam. When the church was young, the Christian community connected the new life of the Resurrection to the new creatures they had become in Baptism; they knew they were the children of God. The connection between their baptism and Good Friday and Easter was so real that they could say with Paul: "We were buried therefore with Him by Baptism into death, so that as Christ was raised from the dead by the glory of the Father, we too might walk in newness of life" (Rom. 6:4). This much they knew to be true from their Easter-baptismal experience: They were "new creatures in Christ."

Hans Reudi Weber, in *The Militant Ministry*, reconstructs how Easter might have been celebrated on the island of Rhodes in the days of primitive Christianity. Just before dawn the Christians and the candidates for Baptism gathered about a large cross carved into a flat rock on top of a mountain. The final questions were asked as the candidates stood on the western side of the cross. As the sun began to rise, each was led down three steps of the western "arm" of the water-filled cross and asked the ancient questions: "Do you believe in God, the Father Almighty . . . and in Jesus Christ, His Son, our Lord . . . and in the Holy Spirit . . . ?" Each person responded three times, "I believe," and each time was completely immersed—"drowned"—in the chilly water of the font. The newly baptized persons went up the eastern "arm" of the cross just as the first rays of the Easter sunrise announced the Day of Resurrection. Confirmation followed and they then joined the community in the celebration of the Easter Communion at the Table of the Lord.

If Weber is at all accurate in his attempt to show what the celebration of the Easter-mystery was like in the early centuries of Christian history, it is safe to conclude that those Christians never forgot their baptismal experience. They knew that they had "died with Christ" in their baptism, which was a kind of burial for them, and they had emerged from the font-tomb into the light and life of a new day. And so their celebration of Easter, as a day when they were "born" into new life as God's children, was extended to every Sunday worship experience; Sunday came to be known as the "little Easter." It has been celebrated ever since as the Day of Resurrection.

Easter is the celebration of God's amazing love for His children and all creation and His mighty power to reverse the order of death and destruction in the world, as shown by His coming out of the tomb in Joseph's garden. (1) New life springs up with Christ's resurrection; He is, indeed, the new Adam after whom God fashions a new race of creatures stamped with the "image of Christ." (2) He rises and takes up life again, and all those who are His will one day erupt from their graves and claim His victorious resurrection-life. The old ways of sin and death have been destroyed forever in Jesus Christ, and we dare to live in hope. Sin cannot destroy us; Christ beat down Satan and sin. And death cannot hold us; Christ conquered it—for Himself and for all of us. We cling to Mark's promise: "He who believes and is baptized will be saved"; we know that the children of God will live forever!

Lent culminated in the death of Jesus Christ, and Ezekiel's question was put for the last time: "Can these bones live?" Easter is God saying to us: "Behold, I will cause breath to enter you, and you shall live. And I will lay sinews upon you, and will cause flesh to come upon you, and cover you with skin, and put breath in you, and you shall live; and you shall know that I am the Lord. . . . Behold, I will open your graves and raise you from your graves, O My people; and I will bring you home into the land of Israel. And you shall know that I am the Lord, when I open your graves and raise you from your graves, O My people. And I will put My Spirit within you, and you shall live. . . . then you shall know that I, the Lord, have spoken, and I have done it, says the Lord" (Ezek. 37:5-6, 12-14).

God spoke on that third day through a heavenly visitor: "He is not here, for He has risen, as He said. Come, see the place where He lay" (Matt. 28:6). God did it: He raised up Jesus Christ, His beloved Son, from the dead; the Spirit has made each believer here alive to God in Christ; and God will one day raise His beloved children to eternal life with Christ in heaven. Alleluia! Amen.

Alive Again

Romans 6:8-11

On a beautiful spring morning, Robert Muller, career diplomat at the United Nations, where he served as an assistant to Dag Hammarskjold, U Thant, and Kurt Waldheim, was walking toward his "beloved little railroad station of Ardley-on-Hudson" in New York when he happened to remember the sad words uttered by a friend the day before. In his book, *Most of All They Taught Me Happiness,* he repeats those words: "My marriage is broken. For some reason that she still has to explain to me, my wife has 'decided' not to love me anymore. All is finished. I feel like gliding into an abyss. You would not believe how everything has changed in my family from one day to another. It is almost unbearable. It is like hell on earth."

Muller decided to make a test and, like the friend's wife, he decided to stop loving nature and dislike it instead. The Hudson River was no longer beautiful; it became, in his imagination, "an ugly mass of water, eternally and boringly renewed for no intelligible purpose." The trees made no sense, the flowers seemed "vain, the crows were killers, the squirrels were vicious, my dreams were illusions, my joy was childish. . . ." Then he looked at himself with dislike: "My job was senseless, my entire life was a wastebasket filled with despair, hopelessness, and death at the end." Muller allowed this new mood to go so far in "its abyss of mud" that, he reports, "I soon felt like vomiting at life, and it suddenly struck me how easy it was to call forth the specter of suicide. I stopped quickly. . . ." He had to shake off the "ugly images" of this dreadful experience in order to regain his accustomed and hopeful stance in life.

The Good Friday experience is behind us but it is not as easily blotted from our memories; the specter of Jesus' death on the cross has been etched into our very beings for as long as we shall live. That experience touches our lives; something of us dies with Jesus Christ—in fact, Paul goes so far in several of his letters as to insist that we have "died with Christ" and have even been buried in His tomb through

Baptism. If that were the complete story of Jesus' life—dead and buried, nothing more—we would have no hope. That's why Paul said to the church at Corinth, "If in this life only we have hope in Christ, we are of all men most miserable." But there is more! Now is Christ raised from the dead and it is this fact that shakes us out of our lethargy and makes us realize that we do have hope. We believe that at the end of time "we shall live with Him." And that belief, confirmed in our rising from the waters of death, means that we are already alive in Christ.

Death Has Lost Its Power

Death hasn't lost its "sting"—we all must pass through its murky depths—but it has lost its power over us. By His resurrection Jesus Christ has changed everything for us. He has rescued us from the tomb from which we had no way out. Before Christ, death was the victor over life, and therefore life really did not make very much sense. Christ confirmed the stories in Scripture about a God who created the world, everything in it, and then made humans in His image as His children. We know that we shall be "lifted up" "live with Him," and that sends us back into life with a real measure of hope.

One of the tragic stories of a recent winter is about a 15-year-old boy hunter who climbed a tree and was "trapped painfully" in it. He could not extricate himself; and his cries for help, as well as shots from his rifle, were not heard. The coroner of Jackson County, Michigan, said, "His leg became wedged in [the tree] and he couldn't free himself. . . . He had a pistol with him and placed it to his forehead, apparently thinking he would never be found." A search party found his body—and it would have reached him in time to rescue him had he not given up hope and pulled that trigger.

Compare that with the story of a man who jumped off a bridge in Minneapolis into the icy waters of the Mississippi River—only to change his mind when the waters were about to claim his life. He reached a piling and called for help. Rescuers threw a rope to him, and he tied himself to the piling so that the current wouldn't wash him away before the three members of the rescue squad of the fire department climbed down ropes to where he was and pulled him out of the water and certain death. Death was thwarted—for a while—in that man's life. The 15-year-old boy is dead; the man was, too, until he was snatched from death's jaws and returned to life once more by the heroic act of the firemen. Life, no matter how bad it was before he entered that water, looked pretty good to him as he felt the power of death grab hold of him; I wonder how it looks to him now. He is alive again—when he ought to be dead.

That's our story—not the first one. Christ has rescued us from the grave, from death. He has set us free from the bonds of the tomb and we are alive again: "Death has no more dominion over us." When Christ effects our rescue at the end of this life, it will be forever. Because He lives, we shall live, too! And that's what we believe—what we dare to hope—and what the memory of our baptism brings to us. We Christians are saved! The Word and the water, through the Holy Spirit, convince us of this, especially in the great fifty days of Easter. Christ is risen! He is risen indeed! This is the great news that breaks into our prisons of fear and death and hopelessness and reverses the whole process of destruction, death, and decay.

Baptism reminds us that we are alive again. Christ set us free from sin and death when it appeared to humanity—up to Christ's death and resurrection—that there was no way out. The late David Roberts once told a story that is unforgettable; it is about a medieval blacksmith who was the strongest man in his city, a careful craftsman, and one of the leaders of the community. The army of a neighboring king captured the city and threw the blacksmith into a dungeon. He was not worried; he could break any chain, bend any bars. He would escape and lead a revolt to free the people in his city. But as he ran his fingers over the chains searching for a weak link, a terrible cry came from his throat. His fingers came upon his secret mark—a kind of trademark—that he put on all his work, and he knew that he could not break those chains; they had no weak link. The only way that he would be freed of them was when his captors, in mercy, came to him and unlocked them—something he could never do for himself. Easter—and our baptism—remind us that God has done just that for you and me. He has set us free in Christ—and that means, even though we must yet pass through death, that we are free indeed! Death holds no fear for us any longer; we are already alive in Christ.

Christ Sends Us Back into the World

Easter and our baptism also remind us that we have become new creatures in Christ—what Paul calls "God's workmanship, created in Christ Jesus for good works, which God prepared beforehand, that we should walk in them" (Eph. 2:10). We are not only alive, but we are "alive to God," which means, to put it another way, that we are "dead to sin" and created to be receptive to the mind and will of God for us and our world. Baptism at Easter reminds us that we are to be new people who live new lives—lives of obedience and responsibility.

One of the people who demonstrates this quality of new life and new responsibilities is one of the A-bomb designers, Theodore B. Taylor, who later concluded that such bombs "were too indiscriminately destructive to be morally justifiable. . . ." (and) he became "increasingly afraid that explosive materials used by government and industry were being inadequately safeguarded." In John McPhee's book, *The Curve of Binding Energy,* his transition "from genius bomber to concerned citizen" is described. A recent story on him announced, "A-bomb designer says future should be solar, not nuclear." He announced last January that he is to become a solar energy contractor. That's similar to the way you and I ought to respond to the realization that we are alive again—new creatures in Jesus Christ—and must live out all the implications of this relationship in the world.

The hope of salvation is only part of the gift that God gives us in Baptism and confirms at Easter as we celebrate the resurrection victory of our Lord. Something dramatic has happened to us in this process God uses to make us His children again—and our response is multi-dimensional in nature. New light comes into our lives to increase our faith and understanding; we are the enlightened ones in Christ. We find ourselves in a new relationship with the Christian community, and we discover new ways to let Christ's love incorporate and direct us into this caring community. As baptized Christians we are expected to do acts of love and service in the world; Christians serve God by serving others. We are charged with the business of witnessing to the Good News in Jesus Christ to all the people in the world. Baptism always has that side to it as the expression of new life in Jesus Christ. If we really are alive again in Christ, we almost automatically ought to set about doing His business in the world with renewed purpose and zeal. To be baptized is to become a servant of the Lord as well as a child of God.

Anything short of doing the good works God planned for us to do is unacceptable among the baptized children of God. We are to be oriented to God and the good, eliminating by positive acts of obedience those elements in our lives which are not pleasing to God nor profitable to others or ourselves. So many of us are lukewarm when it comes to loving obedience to God and the good life, attempting to mix the old ways and the new life together in what we do. Like Thomas Segredi, who could walk among little children in the wards of a children's hospital and bring smiles to the faces of desperately ill children. He started an Operation Happy—a project to arrange for name athletes to visit the children. But William Thomas Segredi had another side; he was a con man who conned people out of money, securities, and such things—and even made them smile while he was robbing them. He was convicted and imprisoned for his crimes despite his good deeds among little children. One day the officials at the prison announced that he had been murdered in his cell. He tried to con the wrong person, apparently, and died for his efforts. The mixture of two radically different ways of life, one so good and helpful, the other so evil and self-serving, resulted in his destruction and death. The same thing happens to those of us who are the children of God if we attempt to live out our baptism with less than total commitment and obedient service.

We have been restored to the garden situation at the time of the creation, and we are given a new chance to live on the earth as God wanted Adam and Eve to live at the beginning. The sentence of death has been lifted. Satan has been taken "off our backs." And this means that we are free again—free to be what we are, God's own children, and to get on with the business that He laid out for humanity when the world was brand new. Christ has made us alive again so that we can go back into the world and live as Christians are supposed to live—in love and service.

Keeping Alive in the Face of Sin

Easter is—for those who know themselves to be God's children in Holy Baptism—a time of high resolution and definitive action. There is a touch of the traditional New Year's resolutions here. We determine that we will run the race as we never have before—and for a time all goes well with us. But before long we find ourselves falling back into the old ways, becoming separated from God once again. For all intents and purposes, we are dead and don't even know it.

The question is just how we can keep "alive to God" and, at the same time, "dead to sin." The answer is that we can't if we try to do it all by ourselves—neither keeping ourselves "alive" nor successfully putting putting down sin in our lives. But God has a message for each of us who, through Baptism, are really "born again" Christians. Jesus spoke it, "Lo, I am with you always, even to the end of the world." He makes Himself available to us whenever we turn and call upon Him. He never fails us, as the history of the church reminds us. The "noble army of martyrs," the saints who died in Christ, called upon Him and were comforted and strengthened by His presence all the way to, and through, death's door.

A "daily dip" in the waters of Baptism—which is a way of saying, repent and return to the Lord each day and He will make you alive again—is where Luther found help. He teaches us that we have to go through this process of dying and rising with Christ every day as long as we live. There is no other way that we can keep alive to God and "slay sin" as it constantly assaults us. Because we are baptized, we can turn and pray to God with confidence, knowing that He is our Father and will sustain us with His love. He hears all of those who come with their needs and pray, "Our Father in heaven. . . ."

A seminary student learned this lesson when he was working in a hospital as a student chaplain. The code for a cardiac crisis sounded and he went to the room as fast as he could. The hospital staff—crash cart and specialized team—was there, desperately at work to save the life of a man having a heart attack. The student asked the hospital chaplain, who got there before he did, if there was anybody in the bed on the other side of the curtain. He answered, "I don't know," so the student looked and saw a terrified man who grabbed his hand and said, "That might have been me." He poured out a story of three heart attacks and strokes—and his body shook as he wept. He was supposed to be the strong person in his household: a rock—self-sufficient, independent, and not needing "anyone's help to live life" confidently. Now he needed help and, unashamedly, called for it for the first time in his adult life.

The student asks, "How often do we ask for help? We talk much about the fact that Baptism places us in a favorable fellowship with God, but we totally fail to state that Baptism places us in a radical relationship to each other. One of the startling realities for me is that if I entrust part of myself to my Christian brothers and sisters, I won't get hurt. . . . Learning how to ask for help means I have to see myself in a different light. . . . I need to remember that God doesn't ask me to be strong, only to remember that He is with me. My dignity is not based on what I do or don't do; it is based on the fact that God in His infinite mercy decided that I was worth loving. . . . If the cross proclaims anything for my existence and yours it is at least that. . . . If nothing can separate us from the love of God, we are free to grow, struggle, and become what the Father in heaven would have us to be."

God sees our difficulties in our struggle to be His children in the world—and He makes Himself available to us when we call upon Him and trust Him. We don't have to worry about keeping ourselves alive, that's God's concern—and He is able to keep His part of the covenant relationship between Himself and us quite well. All of us need to return to our childhood, in a way, and learn that simple faith again into which we were baptized. Do you remember how it goes in that "first hymn" we learned?

> Little ones to Him belong;
> They are weak but He is strong

Yes, indeed, Jesus loves me—loves you and me—for not only the Bible but also, and particularly, my baptism tells me so. And the God who hears and answers our daily prayers for renewal and for strength will keep us alive so that we might be His children and accomplish what He wants us to do in the world. Amen.

Children of Light

Ephesians 5:8-16

San Clemente is in Rome—the original San Clemente. It is two churches built on top of the home and house-church of St. Clement, claimed to be the third bishop of Rome. The Church of St. Clement is but a few blocks away from the Coliseum, an uphill walk because the dirt and debris have collected over the centuries and created a grade that rises to, and beyond, the entrance to the 12th-century church building. A stairway takes visitors to a fourth-century church immediately below the surface building; it has been completely excavated. And another set of stairs takes people down to the level of Clement's home, where, it is claimed, Christians gathered for worship in the first three centuries of Christian history. Additional excavation has revealed a small temple of Mithra, first-century in origin, beyond the one wall of Clement's home. Rival worship services could have been held at the same time—Christians worshiping the risen Christ as children of darkness and heathen offering their bloody sacrifices to gain the favors of their god. The children of darkness, if we may call them that, were wiped out; their place of worship might have been buried forever if Christians had not been interested in uncovering the story of the "children of light." Christians today worship, almost as flowers reach up toward the sun, on one of the very spots, literally above it, where Christians gathered to pray and read Paul's Letter to the Romans and worship their Lord, Jesus Christ. They knew that they were children of light.

The once-great city of Ephesus is built on the side of a hill, and its marble ruins suggest how magnificent it must have been when Paul visited it, preached and taught there, and later wrote a letter to those Christians. Indeed, it was a "city that could not be hid"; its lamps at night must have been visible to ships sailing on the Aegean Sea. It was the city of Diana, or Artemis, who was worshiped and revered by non-Christians living in that "sin city." Paul had to remind the Ephesian Christians they were children of God and therefore children of light, and he urged them to live as children of light, not of darkness. Today all of the Christian buildings lie in ruins, not only in Ephesus but in most of modern Turkey, or they have been turned into museums. There are few children of light left there; a newer religion has replaced them and won over the children of darkness, too—the Muslim faith. Paul's words are seldom read there, but they are read, and we hope heeded, in Rome. Could it be that the Christians in that far-distant land forgot who they were and how they were to live?

Christians Are Children of Light

People who have discovered again that they are children of God in Baptism also need to think of themselves as the children of light. That means, simply, that we not only must know who we are but what sort of people we are and are becoming as Christians. With the resurrection of Jesus Christ the full light of God has illuminated the darkness that enveloped the world on Good Friday and shines upon sinner and saint alike. But only the Christians hear the ancient words that now have been given new meaning: "Arise, shine; for your light has come, and the glory of the Lord has risen upon you. For behold, darkness shall cover the earth, and thick darkness the peoples; but the Lord will arise upon you, and His glory will be seen upon you. And nations shall come to your light, and kings to the brightness of your rising. Lift up your eyes round about, and see. . . . Then you shall see and be radiant, your heart shall thrill and rejoice" (Is. 60:1-5). Christ is risen! Alleluia! The light shines into the darkness and dispels it. The darkness can't snuff it out any more. The light will shine forever—and it will sustain us when we perceive ourselves to be the children of God, children of that Light, Jesus Christ.

The story of Matt Barringer is one of moving from a kind of darkness into the light of a new day because of Eleanor Craig, author of *One, Two, Three, the Story of Matt, a Feral Child*. Matt was considered to be a "wild," or feral child, six years of age when she first met him. He had never walked or talked, nor was he toilet trained, and he couldn't even feed himself. He clung to his mother constantly; doctors pronounced him retarded and untrainable. In desperation, Matt's father called the counseling center in Harrison County, Connecticut; that's how Eleanor Craig became interested and involved with Matt. She discovered that both parents had contributed to the child's difficulties, but especially his mother who was so afraid of the outside world that she never went out. Ms. Craig worked with the child, despite setbacks, in the home, and finally, one day he began counting—the first words he had spoken—as he followed her up a flight of stairs. Gradually he emerged from the darkness of what would have been an institutionalized life for as long as he lived. At age 11 he was able to go to school and enter a fifth-grade class in which he is reading, doing math, and speaking at that level. He has indeed come out of utter hopelessness into the full light of the world. He has an opportunity to live a normal and useful and happy life because Eleanor Craig was perceptive enough and sufficiently loving to recognize his possibilities and work to release him from the darkness. Matt is a child of light—and a kind of grace, too.

From the time that Adam and Eve were expelled from the Garden of Eden, God knew that His children were children of darkness in need of light. He called to His children through Moses and the prophets; He gave them the Law and the promise. Yet His people seemed at times to be hopelessly enslaved in the chains of darkness. Then He sent His Son into the world to redeem His children from the darkness. God's light dawned with Christ's birth, and the brightness of it was revealed in His life and His death until the full power of it was released after His resurrection. John saw this clearly: "He was in the beginning with God; all things were made through Him, and without Him was not anything made that was made. In Him was life, and the life was the light of men. The light shines in the darkness, and the darkness has not overcome it. . . . The true light that enlightens every man was coming into the world. . . . And the Word became flesh and dwelt among us, full of grace and truth; we have beheld His glory, glory as of the only Son from the Father" (John 1:2-5, 9, 14). He could have added Isaiah's word: "Arise, shine, your light has come!" That's what he wants us to see in his Gospel.

One of the most appropriately named Lutheran churches in the world stands across the street from the YMCA in Kowloon. Hundreds of thousands of refugees from mainland China, who settle in Kowloon, the New Territories, and Hong Kong pass by that church and see its sign, in English and Chinese, True Light Lutheran Church. Theirs has been a dramatic escape from a type of darkness into the light of freedom, and by its name the church is extending an invitation to come into, and abide in, the "true" Light of the world, Jesus Christ. The business of that congregation, and all Christians, is to pass on to people in darkness Jesus' message: "I am the Light of the world; he who follows Me will not walk in darkness, but will have the light of life" (John 8:12). Easter affirms that message for us all and forever.

Christians Live in the Light

The children of God have never been permitted simply to stand around and bask in the light God provides in Jesus Christ. They are to live and work in the light provided them by God. This was made abundantly clear when Christ ascended into heaven. According to St. Luke "As they were looking on, He was lifted up, and a cloud took Him out of sight. And while they were gazing into heaven as He went, behold, two men stood by them in white robes, and said: "Men of

Galilee, why do you stand looking into heaven?" (Acts 1:9-11). That was God's way of telling them to get on with the task that had been given them by their Lord. They might have remembered the time when He said: "We must work the works of Him who sent Me while it is day" (John 9:4). They knew, as we all must, that Christ is the Light of the world and we, with them, must know that we live in that light and do His work in it.

When the Apostle Paul says, "Understand what the will of the Lord is" (Eph. 5:17), he is issuing a call to responsible living as children of God in the world. Instead of Luke's message, "Why do you stand looking into heaven," Paul uses a darkness-sleep-wake-up approach to Christian living. To live in darkness is to engage in a "sleep unto death." Christians are to awaken from "the dead" and, with Christ "shining" on them, attempt to discern the nature of their response to God's goodness in Jesus Christ. You and I, as God's children in Christ, need to respond to Paul's urging to be thoughtful people who seek to know "what the will of the Lord is." Our business is never simply to go around saying, "I am saved! I am saved!" or even, "Jesus is Lord." We have God-given responsibilities in His world.

God outlined a simple program of responsibility for all of His people at the creation. And there are signs that we are beginning to exercise "dominion" over the earth in a manner that is pleasing to Him and profitable to all life on this planet. We are becoming conscious of our voracious appetite—especially in America—for the nonrenewable resources of the earth; the energy shortage, whether or not it is really as acute as it seems to be, is upon us and we are beginning to respond intelligently, if not sacrificially. And we are making great strides in caring for the earth—protecting valuable soil from erosion and other damage done to it by the elements. The work of people like Norman Borlaug, winner of the Nobel Peace Prize in 1970 for pioneering in the development of more productive grains to ease world hunger, provides an example of responsible concern that is coupled to positive and intelligent action. Few of us will become scientists of his caliber, but all of us will discover what God wants us to do in the world if we accept the responsibility of being Christian. Responsibility for living and working comes with restoration to fellowship with our Father through Jesus' death and resurrection.

Christians Reject the Darkness

Equally important, if Christians are to live as children of light, is that they, you and I, reject those parts of life that Paul labels darkness: immorality, drunkenness (and he would add drugs today), robbery, murder, and other violence—the things that make up the headlines in

101

our newspapers today. He does not allow us to live in "gray" areas which we tend to frequent and where there is no right or no wrong. A scientist-professor is typical of many of us. In a discussion with friends about the historicity and validity of the Bible he said, "It doesn't really bother me whether or not the Bible is literally true. I live by the Judeo-Christian ethic and morality that has come to me through Scripture." But at the very moment he said this he was living a lie; he was carrying on an "affair" with one of his students and, apparently, believed that what he was doing was compatible with the ethic and morality of the Holy Bible. He really lived by "situation" ethics, which is a way of saying that we make our own guidelines about what is right and wrong *for us*. And if we consider ourselves to be Christians, we attempt, by deceiving ourselves, to construct an extra-Biblical, extra-Gospel, way of life which we adorn with our own stamp of approval by our actions and behavior in the world. Dare we call this "living in the light?"

We reject the darkness when we come to the place where we are able to see ourselves as forgiven sinners. God has lifted the burden of guilt off of our backs, and that means that we are living in the light of God's love. That lights up the darkness and wipes it out.

Jesus Christ is the Light of the world. He lights up the whole world and He dispels the darkness which is too much for us without Him. In the earliest years of the Church's existence, the Easter baptismal service was probably a candlelight service, because it began in darkness. As the Vigil of Easter developed, it became a four-part service: The Service of Light, the Service of the Lessons, the Service of Baptism, and the Holy Communion. It all began in the darkness when flint and iron were used to kindle a new flame, the fire of Easter. Next, the Paschal Candle was lighted—then the candles of the ministers, and the light was passed on to the people so that as the celebrant stopped and chanted three times, "The Light of Christ," the church went from complete darkness to the full illumination offered by the candles all over the nave. That Easter light was kept burning until the next Good Friday. With the resurrection of Jesus Christ the light shines—in all its fullness—in the world again. God's children live by that Light, in that Light—they are the children of light forever.

We are the children of light and the children of God. Amen.

The Inclusive Community

1 Corinthians 12:12-13; 24b-25

Baptism is often called the initiation ceremony of the Christian church. It is just that. We become members of the church, the body of Christ, by water and the Spirit. Baptism announces that we belong to God through Jesus Christ; we have been "signed with the cross." We are part of a very special community—a very exclusive group, in one sense, which receives its uniqueness from God the Father. And yet, though it is exclusive, membership is open to everyone who "believes and is baptized."

Americans are almost inundated with offers of gift memberships to one organization or another. Various auto clubs, book clubs, record and tape clubs fill the daily mail with invitations to join their groups without obligation. Membership in such organizations is quite different than God's gift in Baptism; their "free gift" is generally a "trial" membership with strings attached to it; when the trial period is up, membership is put on a pay-as-you-go basis. And of course, "you may terminate your membership at any time you become dissatisfied" with whatever service is involved. The benefits and privileges are ours as long as we pray for them. None of them gives a free gift that continues for an unlimited period of time. Human institutions can't operate that way. But God does, and Baptism is a demonstration of that gift. God also works mysteriously through His Word and Spirit to move us to accept His gifts in Baptism—forgiveness of our sins, deliverance from death, and belonging to the body of Christ, the church.

A little girl had been adopted by Americans who paid her fare and expenses in being brought to the United States from Korea. She loved them and accepted their style of life without difficulty, despite the fact that she was six years old when she began living with them. She looked forward to going to church school and worship services and participated in them with enthusiasm as she learned the liturgy and the hymns. But she had never been baptized, and she did not want to be baptized, which seemed to contradict her pleasure in attending Sunday school sessions and church services. One day the pastor invited all the children to come forward to the font; he simply told them about the meaning of Baptism, why the special candle was standing by the font. He said, "It means that Jesus is here, even if we can't see Him. He makes us His children by Baptism." The pastor asked the children to remain at the font and participate in the Baptism of a recently born baby. They did. When the little girl got back to her parents, she said, "Now I want to be baptized." Somehow she understood—and she was ready to accept the gift God offered her.

But baptism is inclusive, too, as Paul pointed out to the Corinthian Christians. All the members of the community are involved with each other. They have moved from isolation to integration into a society, a special family, that is marked by love and concern for each other. This is one of the elements in Baptism that causes it to be known as a "rite of passage." We are brought from outside the church into its unique fellowship, so that we may be in communion with God and each other. Baptism does that, too.

Community Responsibilities

In most parts of the Christian church, "private" baptisms are rapidly disappearing. The Sacrament of Holy Baptism is being administered at public services of the church, except for special circumstances usually created by emergency situations. And congregations actively participate in the rites of Baptism—standing, sitting, joining in prayers, creed, and baptismal liturgy—rather than being spectators while the ministers and their assistants "do" all parts of the service. When we do baptisms this way, we are all participating in the "entrance rite" of the church and indicating our acceptance of those baptized in accordance with Jesus' command: "Let the children come to Me; do not hinder them; for to such belongs the kingdom of God. Truly, I say to you, whoever does not receive the kingdom of God like a child shall not enter it (Mark 10:14-15). And Mark reports, "He took them in His arms and blessed them, laying His hands upon them" (v. 16). That's reason enough for our participation in public services of Baptism, isn't it?

We are beginning to comprehend again—because it must have been this way when the church was young—that our "blessing" is a continuing relationship with all of those who are brought into our little portion of the church by Baptism. The ancient questions are still asked of parents and sponsors: "In Christian love you have presented these children for Holy Baptism. You should, therefore, faithfully bring them to the services of God's house, and teach them the Lord's Prayer, the Creed, and the Ten Commandments. As they grow in years, you should place in their hands the Holy Scriptures and provide for their instruction in the Christian faith, that, living in the covenant of their Baptism and in communion with the church, they may lead godly lives until the day of Jesus Christ. Do you promise to to fulfill these obligations?"

Another dimension has been added in many of our congregations today; those baptized are "presented" to the congregation at the conclusion of the baptismal rite. Baptism always adds to the responsibilities of a congregation to provide for and actively participate in the welfare and growth of all those who are received into this inclusive community, the body of Jesus Christ, His church.

These responsibilities begin every time someone is baptized in the name of Father, Son, and Holy Spirit. That's why we pray for them, why we provide schools for their instruction, why we volunteer to teach them in church school or confirmation classes, and why we sponsor the activities of youth groups in our congregations. We belong to an inclusive community—a "mutual concern" kind of society that is this way because Christ has ordained that we should "love each other as He has loved us." Baptism binds us to each other as well as to God in this special way.

A young man once lived with a family whose members really loved and cared for each other, a model Christian family. All were concerned for the welfare of others; each member put the other members' needs above his or her own. Their relationships were based on mutual love, respect, and concern for each other. He said that a plaque in the kitchen summed up the essence of their relationships with each other so well—a translation of 1 Thessalonians 5:11, "Stand by one another, and each one build up the other." This family was a model of what the larger community, the church, should be like in the relationships of all its members. Baptism lays this model upon us all.

A Loving Community

Congregations as Christian communities are able to fulfill their responsibilities to each other and the world because Christian love is the foundation of what they are. Truly, as a popular hymn declares, "They will know we are Christians by our love." It was that way in the first century. Non-Christians looked at the Christians in utter amazement: "See how these Christians love one another," they said. They were genuinely concerned about each other's fortunes and welfare. They were willing to die for each other, as well as live for one another, because they were acutely aware of the gifts that God had given them— the world, the wonder of life, the care of the earth, and the nurture of those for whom we have responsibility. The Christian community witnesses to its uniqueness by what it is, and it teaches its members by the quality of its concern and its care for others, reflecting how much God loves us all.

Love is constructive, edifying, and up-building in us, and through us, because love is God's power at work in us and the world. His love constrains us from being the sort of people who destroy rather than build up other people; it is our responsibility to love as God loves us. When love is extended to others by what we are and what we do, they comprehend their worth, their uniqueness, in our eyes and in the eyes of God. All persons learn best what they really are when other persons show them by their care and consideration that they are loved.

Our responsibility toward each other is to reflect the love of God in us by the ways we live with people baptized into this same community, in all situations and under all circumstances.

A young man in a neighboring community was accused of the heinous murder of a 13-year-old girl. His parents could not believe he would do such a thing, but people in their community apparently did. They made the week after the young man's arrest "hell here on earth," according to his mother. His father was harassed at his work and at home by "friends and strangers alike," according to members of the family; he had a heart attack and "died of a broken heart." His accused son stood "by his bier" on the day that the girl he was suspected of slaying was buried. The day before his heart attack and death, he spoke to his son and reassured him of his love. People sent their "hate" letters to the newspapers as well as to the parents, but one letter, an anonymous one, was different: "I plead with the people in this state to try to understand. . . . You raise a child, you hope that you have raised him well, yet he and only he can decide what he will do with his life. No one is responsible for another man's acts. Stop condemning those who are related by blood. There is only one family who grieves more than [the family of the accused man] over LoAnn's death—her own family." But that expression of love did not come in time to reassure the father of that man in jail. He was destroyed by hate when he and his wife should have been surrounded by love and concern and care when they needed it so desperately. Love might have saved him from the heart attack and death, if enough expressions of love had reached him from the community around him and the people of the church. To show people our love—and to tell them of it, too—is our responsibility as God's children in the world.

Love Is Perceived by the World

In one of the "Marcus Welby, M.D.," episodes, a once-great but now down-and-out motion picture director had to be hospitalized in an institution provided by people in the motion picture industry for anyone in the "business" who might need financial assistance in time of illness. He was a cardiac patient, ultimately underwent successful open-heart surgery, and made a comeback in the motion pictures by producing a "hit" film that he had made but never released. One scene in the TV drama saw the camera clearly in focus on another wall plaque—this one behind a reception desk: "We take care of our own." Sometimes that's what the world sees when it looks at the Christian community, and its logical conclusion is that Christians don't really care for people who might be outside the church of Christ.

When Jesus said, "You are the light of the world," He added: "Let your light so shine before men, so that they may see your good works and give glory to your Father who is in heaven" (Matt. 5:14-16). People in the world will notice how we behave toward each other—and toward them, too—when we live in the love of God. Love expands our horizons beyond "we take care of our own" so that all people are taken into our circle of concern. When a pastor inadvertently walked into a church basement where an elaborate reception was underway, because he was "dressed like a bum" at the end of a week-long experiment in living with down-and-out persons in Chicago, he was asked what he wanted. "I'm hungry," he said, looking at the sumptuous buffet on the other side of the room; "I haven't had anything to eat since yesterday." A man replied, "We don't offer that kind of service here. The Salvation Army has a soup kitchen down the street. Go down there, and they'll feed you." The pastor recognized the man; he had been on a pulpit committee that had interviewed him five years before and had recommended that the congregation call him as pastor. "Don't you know me? You called me as your pastor a few years ago." He told them enough about himself that he convinced the people who had gathered around him that he was indeed the man who might have been their pastor had he accepted their call. Then they quickly invited him to help himself to some food, but he responded, "No thank you, I think I'll go down the street." When we take "care of our own" in the Christian community, it must be in such a way that it attracts the world and intrigues people to wonder how we can be this way toward each other instead of shutting them out. Then they might ask how they may join this special community—because the nature of our love tells them that they belong there, too.

That's the kind of community that Christ created through Word and Spirit after his resurrection from the dead, and Baptism is our initiation into it. Our love for God and one another is the sign that we really belong in it. Love always identifies us as the children of God through Christ the Lord. Amen.

Fifth Sunday of Easter

Servants of God

Luke 3:3-9; see also 2 Corinthians 6:3-10

Baptism, as John the Baptist understood it, is an act wherein God washes away the sins of those who "repent and are baptized"; and he connected his baptism to the coming of the Promised One of God. We can understand that much about his message that was preached so urgently and convincingly. John understood that the Messiah was about to make His appearance and he did "prepare the way" for the coming of the Holy One of Israel. Most of us miss or overlook the fact that John called on those repentant sinners who were baptized to lead a new kind of life: "Bear fruits that befit repentance." And true to his conception of his mission and message, he warned his hearers that "every tree therefore that does not bear good fruit is cut down and thrown into the fire." The baptism of John called for God's people to become active servants when they came up out of the waters of the Jordan. They had to be profitable to God.

As John preached repentance, it required people to return to the Lord, be baptized for the forgiveness of their sins, and also "produce the appropriate fruits" of repentance and Baptism. From his perspective forgiven sinners must become servants of God. No longer are they to be self-serving persons whose priorities in life revolve around themselves; now they are to please God and serve the Lord for the rest of their lives. Given new life through our Baptism, we too have become and must be the servants of God, who also "produce appropriate fruits" by what we do in life.

Ordination for Service

Restoration to a relationship with God as His children carries with it a renewal of the responsibilities given to people in the garden by our Creator-God. Baptism makes us children of God again, so that we might continue to live in that relationship as we look forward to that final hope promised us by Christ, salvation. We are renewed by water and the Spirit so that we might live in love and faithfulness. Our baptism, therefore, is a kind of "ordination" that lays a "yoke of service" over the shoulders of each one of us. We are all to be priests and ministers, not of Word and sacraments in all cases, but as those who serve God in awareness of their relationship with Him. Some of us are called to the ordained ministry of preaching, teaching, and sacramental acts, but every one of us is called to be a servant of the living God. Such service issues from new life.

An intelligent young man, a pastor's son, often talked about being called to the pastoral ministry; he seemed almost certain to enter the seminary but altered his vocational course and prepared for work in another field of professional service. When he told his decision to his father, he was asked: "What happened to your call to Christian ministry?" And the son replied, "I heard you say many times in your sermons that God has called every one of us to be His servants—and in whatever vocation we may choose to enter. I believe that I will be able to serve God without becoming a pastor." And he pursued his course of preparation, completed it, and is doing just that. God wants all of His people not only to love Him but to serve Him. Baptism lays that kind of a responsibility—a sort of lay ordination—upon every single one of us who claim to be His children in Christ.

To be servants of God is a high calling, indeed. Every person who does his/her best to be "profitable to the Lord" is equally valuable to God. All God asks of us is that we serve Him faithfully and to the best of our ability. And that's where difficulties develop, because it is too impractical in our kind of a world always to be working for God and the Kingdom. Life demands too much of us; making a living is a nearly all-consuming activity for many of us. Who can put God first in all things that are done each day? That's not only impractical, but it goes against the spirit of our times. The world constantly conditions us to "think about ourselves," to "put ourselves first," that "we're the ones that count" and that "we deserve everything we can get out of life." If we believe the messages that bombard our senses and our minds, there is precious little of our time, energies, or efforts that may be devoted to God, is there?

Not that there is a dearth of opportunities to serve God! They are all around us; they, too, assault us and demand consideration and positive action, if we consider ourselves to be Christians. It may take a bit of imagination to discover how we can become profitable servants of God when the needs are so great and our talents and abilities seem so limited. Some time ago, national attention was focused on a man living in Richmond, Va., who earned only $16,000 a year as a postal worker but had become a philanthropist. In the last five years, this man has given away over $33,000 to people he has read about who are in need or have done some good deed. He and his wife deprive themselves of most luxuries—a television set and a telephone are the exceptions—and have allowed their roof to leak, their siding to need paint, and their electrical wiring to be dangerously obsolete in order to "free [their] money to do these other things." Since 1972, he has helped a 9-year-old boy from South America who needed heart surgery; a black couple who have been foster parents to more than 40 children in the last 15 years; a former boxer who works with "street waifs"; a 14-year-old boy who found $25 on the school bus and returned it, only to be taunted by his schoolmates; an Egyptian youth in need of an abdominal operation. Countless other people are his beneficiaries.

That people should find the actions of Thomas Cannon peculiar— for that is the philanthropist's name—is understandable. People of average means just don't live that way in America. He has been scoffed at by his coworkers and hounded by people seeking his favors. Publicity given to his deeds threatens his life and that of his family from "criminal elements." Some have said that this is his way of "playing God" on a small scale—but it is merely his way of being a servant of God and His people. He sends a letter with each check—and that's what counts to him: "It's not the amount of money that's important, it is the amount of caring it symbolizes. The thoughts expressed in my letter usually become more important to the recipients than the amount of money." When people really care about God and each other, they find all sorts of ways to become servants and fulfill their obligations to their Lord and those whom He has redeemed.

From Self-centered to Other-centered Living

New life in Jesus Christ means that the center of our lives has shifted from concern and care for ourselves to acts of love and mercy done regularly and spontaneously for others. The recognition and acceptance of this "burst of new life" in us prompts us every day to respond to this new thing that God has done in Jesus Christ with renewed praise and thanksgiving. This is the impetus that impels us to virtually throw our lives away for Christ and the Gospel—and the sake of others, of course. Grateful response to God's gifts ought always to stir us up, as we worship in public and private, and cause us to express that deep emotion in concretely visible deeds in life. New life can't be bottled up inside us or restricted to acts of devotion and worship; it forces its way to the surface of our beings and demands expression in our relationships with God's people.

Jory Graham, a journalist living in Chicago is a cancer victim who writes a column, "A Time for Living." She writes and lives "under the shadow of death." Her cancer is in remission for now, but she seems to demonstrate the quality of grateful response to whatever "extended life" she has received by ministering to others through her column and other activities. She writes about people who, like her, have been victims of cancer but have found the power to cope with it. One of her stories is about Stephen Henderson, who was given up for dead in 1965; kidney disease was almost fatal then—dialysis was new, transplants experimental. But he heard that the Medical College of Virginia in Richmond had an experimental transplant center. He had to sign papers before his transplant: "This person is terminally ill. He is going to die. This transplant is strictly experimental. There is no other hope." He lived—and is still alive—and living a grateful and productive life. He and his wife have created a nonprofit Full Circle Counseling Service (birth to death is the full circle); it takes them everywhere in the country, so they sold their home and live in a van. They counsel people in any kind of death "situation"—and their services are "free" to those who are dying.

Jory Graham writes: "I want you to know about the Hendersons because they offer a unique service in America that deserves our support. With warmth and gentleness, they give what we in deep trouble need most: loving concern, tremendous understanding, techniques for pain relief, and most of all, hope." They may be humanitarians—I don't know about their faith—but they are living the way that Christians ought to live in the light of the Easter event when the whole world resounds with "Christ is risen. Alleluia!" And in our hearts and with our lives, when we comprehend what that means for life in time and eternity, we respond, "He is risen, indeed!"

The people living in our world need the ministrations and the witness of us Christians who claim to have found new life in Jesus Christ. People all over the world literally bombard our senses with their cries for help, for a chance to live. We become so used to seeing the starving and the desperate that we become hardened to their plight. The picture of a boat absolutely packed with people—not a place for anyone to move—arriving in Miami from Haiti gets only a passing glance and an, "Oh, more refugees for us to take care of." Who thinks about a picture like that long enough to realize that we wouldn't even ship cattle crowded together as those human beings are? So often, it takes an organized effort, with publicity, plan, and program, to stir us into action that ought to be a natural and normal dimension of Christian life.

People need us and what we can do for them as their brothers and sisters just as much as we, when confronted by sin and death, need the might and merciful God. We also need to know that people need us, too. The famous French worker-priest, Abbe Pierre, discovered that early in his ministry. He had been ill, was feeling totally inadequate and despondent when the police called him to a run-down hotel in his slum-situated parish in Paris to minister to a man who had tried to kill himself. The priest looked down at him and said, "My poor fellow, how am I expected to help you when I am in such desperate need of help myself?" The man answered, his eyes showing his interest: "Father, do you mean to say that there might be on this earth someone more miserable than I, someone who might need my help?" And Abbe Pierre says: "His words were a revelation to me. They aroused me from my lethargy. His message was that man's greatest need was to be needed by others, to be of service to others. . . . While he spoke, I could suddenly visualize the multitude of poor fellows like him who were craving to be of help to others in the world, who wanted to be full, useful human beings and to be part of the celebration of life. Nobody, I thought to myself, should ever be allowed to fall as low as not to be needed by someone else. . . . What could I do for them? An idea suddenly arose in my mind: Why not get together with other shipwrecks like him and do something for people still poorer and more miserable than ourselves?" The two of them, then and there, founded the Disciples of Emmaus, to help people to become useful and alive, real people in the world. Isn't that the immediate blessing that God gives us at Easter and in our Baptism?

Robert Muller, who reported Abbe Pierre's story in his *Most of All, They Taught Me Happiness,* says, "I never met again this remarkable man, the son of a wealthy silk merchant of Lyon, who had chosen for his earthly destiny the company and the path of the poor. . . . [but] I never forgot this evening and his inspired words. How many times did they come back to my mind during my life!"

"Feed My lambs," said Jesus before He ascended to the Father, "Tend My sheep." That, indeed is what we are called upon to do, too, and driven by the Spirit of new life, to be His thankful and obedient servants. The needs of other people, as they surface visibly in our lives, tell us that we are needed by them, as well as by God.

Baptism Involves Us in Service

Through our baptism we are involved with all others in our community and outside of it. Again and again in our lives that question Jesus put to His disciples comes back to haunt you and me: "Are you able to drink the cup that I drink, or be baptized with the baptism with which I am baptized?" (Mark 10:38). Few of us have to suffer the same kind of fate Jesus' involvement with God and people thrust upon Him, but all of us are expected to serve sacrificially, as the needs of others involve us in their lives and they become involved in ours. Baptism makes us what we are, and the sign of the cross shapes our response to God's love in Christ in the face of human need. God needs us to do acts of love, mercy, and kindness that not only relieve pain and suffering, but that serve as living witnesses to His grace in Jesus Christ and to His deep concern for us all.

Because we are involved in Christ's mission on earth and because we know that people need us—literally can't get along without us and our love and help—we may dare to live gratefully, generously, sacrificially all the days of our lives. And it might just be that our lives will be the witness that effectively communicates to them the wonder of God's love that is made available in Christ. Loving and obedient service to others confirms our discipleship with Christ, our love for Him and His for us. Cardinal Suhard once said: "To be a witness does not consist in engaging in propaganda, nor even in stirring people up, but in being a living mystery. It means to live in such a way that one's life would make no sense if God did not exist." Living out our baptism in hope and service is an announcement to the world that God does exist, that the risen Christ is Lord of all, and that living in harmony with Him and for Him is the only thing that makes real sense in this world. Amen.

Sixth Sunday of Easter

Mandate for Mission

Mark 16:14-20

In the TV movie of Ray Bradbury's *Martian Chronicles*, not much was made of the fact that in the story the Episcopalian priests Father Peregrine and Father Stone were sent to Mars about three and a half years after the first American attempt at colonization ("November 2002—The Fire Balloons") to minister to the colonists who had settled on Mars during that time. In the book Bradbury's intention is clearly geared to ministering to people who desperately need help to face the problems of daily life. Long before the social upheaval of the 1960s Bradbury emphasized that the church needs to be a serving community that would by its deeds address the needs of people on earth. And so in the book, Father Peregrine, leader of the missionary expedition, asks: "Should we go at all? Shouldn't we solve our own sins on earth? Aren't we running from our lives here?" He completed what almost amounts to an indictment of the church by describing Father Peregrine: "He arose, his fleshly body, with the rich look of strawberries, milk, and steak, moving heavily. . . ." and the mission to Mars shortly thereafter gets under way. Both book and TV "special"—once the missionaries are on Mars—play up the search for the exotic Martians, who are like "blue flames" or "fire balloons," and they dramatize the encounter with the "ancient ones" on Mars who have no need of them. The worldwide, universal mission of the church to preach the Gospel to all people was wiped out.

Toward the very end of His time on earth, Christ clearly outlined the uncompleted task that was to be entrusted to His disciples on earth until He returned again. Mark reports that Christ commanded: "Go into all the world and preach the Gospel to the whole creation." Henceforth, their responsibility was to declare that God had reversed the tragedy that took place in the garden; He had restored His children to fellowship with Him and renewed the "covenant of creation"—"Behold, I make all things new." That's the sort of news we need to hear—and the world needs to hear, too. Through the preaching of the Word and the response

114

of people in Baptism, the people of the world would be saved and join in the continuing mission of telling the story to those who haven't heard it. And the disciples, according to Mark, went out as He ordered them to, and they "preached everywhere," and the Lord was with them.

Christ Cares About the People in the World

Jesus lived and died and rose from the grave for the sake and salvation of every creature who has lived, or does live, on planet earth. He commanded His followers to continue His mission of showing people that God loves them. As Christ cared for the people of His day, so we must be concerned enough about humans, especially in loneliness, pain, and suffering, to do something about their plight. Whenever newspapers carry a headline like Colman McCarthy's, "A 'John Doe' dies of cold; few care," the church ought to remember that the Lord cares and we as His disciples care.

McCarthy reported that on the coldest day of the winter about 30 of Washington, D.C.'s destitute gathered outdoors to bury one of their dead. A horse-drawn cart, carrying the body of a man who lived homeless and died nameless, moved through the streets of Washington. The man froze to death in an empty building only a mile from the White House. This "John Doe" was one "of about 20 others of the wretched and forgotten who have died during the last three winters in Washington's alleys and gutted tenements." Colman McCarthy insists it is much the same in other cities around the country. And that's only a small part of the problem and the Christ-given responsibility placed before the church that bears His name and carries on His mission.

To be new creatures reconciled to the Father through the Son means that new life is throbbing through us. A sense of joy and thanksgiving is fundamental to it; it means renewal of our ability to love, a fresh beginning to the business of caring for the world and God's creatures, which is more than acting like humanitarians out of an impulse to show mercy and loving-kindness upon poor and unfortunate persons in the world. Julius K. Nyerere, President of Tanzania, in a speech given in the United States, said: "Poverty is not the real problem of the modern world. . . . We have the knowledge and resources . . . to overcome poverty. The real problem—the thing which creates misery, wars and hatred among men—is the division of mankind into rich and poor." Later on in the speech, he added: "What does this mean for those who give their lives to the service of the church? First, it means that kindness is not enough; piety is not enough; and charity is not enough." All of the earth's poor "need to be helped to take control of their lives." They need what the Africans call their "unhuru"—their extended family—to help and encourage them because they honestly care for

115

them "in the name of Jesus Christ." Toward the end of the address he asked: "If God were to ask the wretched of the earth who are their friends, are we so sure that we know their answer?" (From *Man and Development*, by Julius K. Nyerere).

Real love for people expresses itself by seeing that their need for community and fellowship are addressed by all of us in the Christian church. They need to know that we help them and care for them because we love them the way that God loves them. And until they know that—whether they are physically hungry or full—they belong to those who hunger and thirst for God's righteousness.

John clearly saw the command of Christ to tell the Good News to the world in terms of "feeding" people as a response to God's love for us in Jesus Christ. After the Resurrection, when Christ surprised Peter and the other disciples on the shore of the Sea of Galilee, and had breakfast with them, He took Simon aside and asked him, "'Simon, son of John, do you love Me more than these?'" Peter answered, "'Yes Lord; You know that I love You.' [Jesus] said to him, 'Feed My lambs.' A second time He said to him, 'Simon, son of John, do you love Me?'" He replied, "'Yes, Lord; You know that I love You.' [Jesus] said to him, 'Tend My sheep.' Then He said to him the third time, 'Simon, son of John, do you love Me?'" Peter was upset that He asked him the third time, "Do you love Me?" and said, "'Lord, You know everything; You know that I love You.' Jesus said to him, 'Feed My sheep'" (John 21:15-17). That's why the oldest mosaics of the risen and ruling Christ show four streams of water issuing from beneath the throne—the four Gospels—combining to form a river with lush grass growing on its banks. The sheep are there eating that rich grass, the Word of life that the church feeds them with, out of love for Christ and a genuine sense of caring for them. By Jesus' resurrection we are new creatures who love enough to do as He commands: "Go into all the world; and preach the Gospel to the whole creation." The Gospel is no handout to the hungry, no act of human kindness; it is the assurance of God's love for all in the death and resurrection of Jesus Christ.

Christlike Persistence in Proclaiming Good News

The world is sending powerful signals to the church of Jesus Christ today in many parts of the world: "We don't need you. We don't want you. Go home and stay home. We have our own gods, and they are as good as your Christ." The resurgence of old religions all over the world is one way that this message is being sent to the Christian church. A pastor and his wife saw this in the new territories outside of Hong Kong and Kowloon on a visit to a Shinto shrine. A funeral had just been held and the artifacts were much in evidence—paper houses to represent the life and possessions of the dead person, the "bridge" that people pass over from life to death to life, along with other symbols to be burned. The open-air altar chambers were lined with pictures of the dead; the altars were laden with sacrifices—food from the living for the dead. Before one of the altars, a Chinese mother was teaching her child, a four-or five-year-old girl, the proper way to do obeisance to their gods. Beyond the temple was a lovely picnic area, and much in the fashion of many American churches today an old people's home was attached to the rear of the temple; it was of considerable size. The message seemed to be: "The old ways and the old gods are good enough for us. We will trust in our prayers, our sacrifices, in life and in the face of our death." If they had heard the Good News—and remember that 3½ billion of the 4½ billion people on earth have not—they rejected it and clung to their traditional faith, that quite often has been reformed to meet contemporary needs of body and soul.

It would seem, according to Kenneth Dale's *Circle of Harmony*, that the Japanese are more impressed with Christian organizations and their programs than they are with the Gospel of Jesus Christ. Dale's book is about one of the "new religions," Rissho Kozekai, that have sprung up in the last 40 years or so and are growing rapidly. R.K., as it is called, is a neo-Buddhist faith of 4½ million members with headquarters in Tokyo. The buildings are impressive in size and number; the main building, with its gigantic statue of Buddha, is used for worship and group discussion known as "hoza." The members are organized into neighborhood groups after the "shepherding" plan used in many American congregations. They meet as groups for worship and "hoza" on the three flat-floored balconies surrounding the church-auditorium; they sit on the floor in circles with their belongings in front of them and talk about their problems in living, under the guidance of a trained leader. The numbers of people who participate in "hoza" are proof positive of the effective role that R.K. plays in their lives.

The message is additionally amplified in Japan as it comes from non-Christian movements like R.K. to the churches: "Your programs and procedures are valuable. We will take them, improve upon them, and use them to revive our religions. Thank you, but we don't need your Christ and your other Christian ways." In the face of this rather friendly resistance, Christians need to persist and proclaim the Good News in love and in ways that will make a deeper impact upon non-Christian people. If we learn from the world that the Gospel is not important to them, perhaps it is because we have been unintentionally propagating something less than the Good News to them. It is time to listen and examine ourselves in the face of Christ's continuing command to the church: "Go into all the world and preach the Gospel to the whole creation." And although it may be difficult to preach and witness to indifferent or uninterested people in our world, we try to be faithful and preach with persistence wherever we may go.

Return to the Resurrection Water

American Christians ought to be comforted and encouraged, on the other hand, by the eagerness with which people in Africa hear the Word today and embrace the faith. The Christian church is growing rapidly in most parts of Africa, so that its story sounds like the story of Christians in the first century. On a recent visit to the United States, Bishop Erasto Kweka described a confirmation service in his diocese. Six hundred and twelve boys and girls were confirmed at a six-hour service; over 4,000 persons literally covered a hillside to participate in the worship service. Thousands of them received Communion with the confirmands. And Bishop Kweka said, "That was only the first service. All in all, over 1,000 young people were confirmed at the two confirmation services." God must be "working with them" just as Mark says that He did when the disciples began to preach.

But the growth of the church in Africa is disturbing when we learn of the difficulties faced and conquered in preaching the Word and witnessing to the power of the Christian faith. Tales of the willing sacrifices made by people and pastors in order to preach the Good News abound. Soon after Bishop Kweka was elected to office, the car that went with it was sold and a smaller, more economical and less ostentatious one was purchased. Asked about the change, he asked, "How could I drive into villages where my pastors don't even have motorcycles?" Many of them are getting around on foot, and some of them, since cars and gasoline are prohibitively expensive, are even riding donkeys on their pastoral rounds. Perhaps that makes another story of a Man riding into Jerusalem upon a donkey to His death more credible.

The resistance we encounter at home and in distant lands as we attempt to preach the Good News to people over against the amazing acceptance of the Word and affirmation of the Gospel in other parts of the world sends us back to Easter, and to our Lord's command, "Go . . . and preach the Gospel to the whole creation." At the font and empty tomb we find forgiveness for our uncertainty and failures and with that forgiveness a new sense of commitment to the mandate for mission that He has laid upon us all. Christ is still alive, and He is very active in the world! Suddenly, we find that He has given us a new "heart" and boldness to obey Him and preach the Gospel fearlessly and with new resolve and purpose.

Every Sunday is a "little Easter" with an invitation built in to return to the Source of our life and mission, Jesus Christ the risen Lord, and at font and table discover a new beginning in mission. Father Gerard Sloyan would remind us as we return to our task: "With you . . . there is the reiterated pledge of fidelity to the promises of your infancy, or whenever you were baptized. You intensify the life of the baptized by giving a fresh and explicit testimony to your faith in Christ. You declare yourselves martyrs, witnesses." And he adds, "A risen life is the best witness to the resurrection of our Lord, in whom we live." It also gives credence to the Word we declare to be Good News in Jesus Christ the Lord.

We might think of this return and renewal in the "little Easter" of every Sunday as a kind of "water power." It may occur over and over again—in fact, it has to; we need to return to the source of our lives in Christ, the waters of Baptism, and do it again and again in order to fulfill Christ's "mandate for mission" as His body, the church, here on earth. And as we preach and witness with fidelity and zeal, with love for Him and His people, trusting in Him to produce results, we may hope to hear Him say to us, "Well done, good and faithful servants . . . enter into the joy of your Master" (Matt. 25:24). So we will know again that we are the children of God—because He has done this for us all. That's Good News, and we will just have to go on sharing it with the whole world while there is time. Amen.

Ascension

The Joyful Departure

Luke 24:44-53

The ascension of Jesus Christ 40 days after His resurrection adds another episode to the events of Good Friday and Easter. Intellectual difficulties in believing that a dead Man could rise from His grave on the third day are compounded by the story that He "ascended to heaven" after He had been seen and heard as the risen Lord. People say, as some always have, that this is just too much to believe because it goes against natural law and the scientific evidence that supports it. People say that there is just no way that a person can launch himself into space without some sort of propulsive device. And, people say, where would a person go if such an ascension were possible; the universe no longer seems like heaven in an age when space exploration has been carried out and people from planet Earth have managed to land—and complete limited exploratory and scientific missions—on the moon.

One of the most impressive "tours" that any human being is able to take any place on the surface of this planet is Cape Kennedy in Florida. Visitors may drive for miles and miles on the tour buses and see the history of space technology unfolded before their eyes. The reception center offers films, lectures, explanations, and exhibits all designed to help visitors understand what they will actually see out on the launching pads. In one spot there is a collection of the various rockets that the United States has developed and launched in the last quarter century. One sees launching pads used for the various "series" and now abandoned and left to break up with time. If one's timing is right, a rocket ready for launching might be seen, or one being assembled in the giant assembly building. Such a tour expands on what we have all seen on our TV screens—an actual launching of a manned rocket, the landing on the moon, or the first pictures sent back from Mars with the successful landings of the unmanned Mariners I and II.

On top of the Mount of Olives, across from the "stoned up" Golden Gate in the walls of Jerusalem, stands a strange little building that marks the traditional site of the ascension of the Lord. The souvenir sellers are there, hawking their wares; the cameldriver and his camel are there for photographing with the tourists. People may buy slides of the building, or of Jerusalem and its holy places, and even of the stone inside the building with its indentation said to have been made by Jesus' foot when He took off from the earth into heaven. That "launching pad" is worlds away from those in Florida or Russia, where successful space flights are always taking place; it taxes one's powers of belief because it goes beyond credibility. More importantly, the ascension of Christ does not have to be proved for Christians; it is at the heart of the Gospel and a tenet of the faith: "He ascended into heaven and is seated at the right hand of the Father," as we declare in our creeds.

A Joyful Departure

The ascension of the Lord is a difficult event for us to believe simply because we live in a scientific age and can't comprehend how it could have taken place; we have learned so much about space in the last three decades which further complicates the problem by adding a "where did He go?" dimension to it. But it is the reaction of the disciples that really ought to catch our attention. After the Lord disappeared from their sight, they were "full of joy." That's so different from their reaction to His first departure—His death—on Good Friday. Then they were shattered, and they couldn't even believe the "good news" about His resurrection. Mark mentions, for instance, that they were mourning and in tears when Mary of Magdala told them that Jesus was alive. They didn't believe her, and they didn't believe the two to whom He appeared "as they were walking into the country." The disciples had seen their Friend die, and they just couldn't believe that He was alive until He appeared to them. When they saw Him, heard Him speak, touched Him, ate with Him, they were convinced; and Luke says, "Their joy was so great that they still could not believe it, and they stood there dumbfounded" (Luke 24:41 JB). Incredibly, when He ascended and departed from them again, they "were full of joy."

The difference in their emotional reaction was simply that they had been changed by the appearances of Christ; they could believe Him now—even when He told them that after He went away they would "be baptized with the Holy Spirit," who would give them the power to carry on His mission. They hadn't known why He had to die; it was beyond their comprehension—but they were joyful because they now both understood and could believe Him when He told them that He would return at the appointed time. All of their experiences with Jesus had prepared them for this moment when, after His return to the Father, they would carry on His mission until He came back to bring in the fullness of the kingdom over which He would reign for all time.

About 25 years ago a congregation erected a new church building that attracted the attention of architects and art lovers. The design was contemporary and utilitarian; the appointments were tasteful and well designed. The building contained interesting art as well. But a cutout area was left in the wall behind the altar-table; it was to contain a mosaic of the ascension of Christ which would be executed when the congregation raised the necessary funds for the project. But by the time the money to complete the mosaic was available, the congregation had decided on another theme for the mural because they realized that the return of Christ might be a better scene behind the table where they pray, "Come, Lord Jesus, come quickly." They couldn't agree on how that theme might be executed realistically in the space that was available; the congregation wanted to declare their belief in Jesus' second coming but they couldn't imagine how it should be done on the wall of their building. Finally someone suggested one word "Maranatha"—their prayer for Christ's return, and they put that one-word mosaic above their altar-table. The ascension of Christ is a promise that He will return again, and that makes the festival a joyous celebration for God's children.

The Ascension Begins Jesus' Reign

The astounding news of Easter morn is incomplete without, and until, the ascension of Christ "to the Father." The Ascension is the last part of the "raising up" of Christ by the Father; it announces that the Lord has been glorified by God—and that is reason for rejoicing. And we sing:

> Laud, honor, and praise to the Lamb that was slain,
> Who sitteth in glory and ever shall reign.

That's what has been imbedded in the walls or ceilings above the altars of many Christian church buildings—the risen and ascended Christ sitting on a throne, hand upraised in blessing, Peter and Paul on either side of Him, and the "host of heaven" behind and above Him. There is nothing of Michelangelo's "Last Judgment" painting on the altar-wall of the Sistine Chapel. Rather, the "Christ in glory" mosaic motif suggests that the Christ is overseeing His business being done in the world by His people and that those who call Him Lord and do His work have nothing to fear now nor at the end of time when He returns as promised.

The Lord has disappeared from the sight of the world, but it has always been understood, in the Ascension, that He is very much alive. His final "raising up" was never understood in terms of death, destruction, or disintegration; because it affirms that everything about Him and His life and His teachings is true. God lifted Him up and glorified Him, "the beloved Son," as the affirmation, endorsement, and conclusion of all God wanted Him to do on earth. But Christ's ascension has always meant, too, that He is free from the bondage of body, time, and space; and that's partly why the believers have always placed the risen, ascended Lord above their altar-tables. The Christ who is risen and reigning at the right hand of the Father is able to be present "when two or three are gathered together in [His] name." He is able to be the Host at the table-feast he ordered His disciples and followers to observe. The Lord is alive—He lives! He is "high and lifted up" but able to be with His own, feeding them, encouraging them in their work, and supporting them in all the crises of life. That living and ascended Lord shares in, and adds to, the joy of all the occasions when His people gather to celebrate any aspect of their lives—from birth to death—with Him. The ascension of the Christ clearly announces that, in glory, He is able to complete His promise, "Lo, I am with you always, to the close of the age" (Matt. 28:20).

Just think of the effect of the death and Resurrection, the Ascension and Pentecost, upon the disciples of Christ. They really were changed persons, and not merely because they were able to believe what they had actually seen; they were able to "take up their crosses daily, and deny themselves, and follow their Lord" into the world and to their own terrible deaths. The disciples had run away when Jesus was arrested in the garden, watching His execution from a distance—the exception, of course, was John. Peter had enough courage to attend part of Jesus' trial, but when asked whether or not he was a disciple, he denied vehemently that he even knew Jesus. After the Resurrection and Ascension Peter and all the rest of the disciples were bold and fearless, literally throwing away their lives—for the Lord and His Gospel. Without the sense of His presence and His power they would not have changed so radically or been like this. Death had been defeated by Christ forever.

In his book *The Medusa and the Snail* Dr. Lewis Thomas titles one chapter, "On Natural Death." He believes that the body has a mechanism that "turns off" pain when the final stages of terminal illness set it, especially in cancer cases. From his perspective, the "death and dying" courses so popular in sacred and secular community alike are almost unnecessary. Death is natural; its processes take over and "assist" people to die, often pain free and fearlessly. But the church informs people that they need not fear death because death has been defeated and eternal life is a reality for those who believe that Jesus Christ is Lord. That's God's ultimate gift to His children through Christ—a present reality and a future promise—and that's what frees us up so that we may live faithfully and fearlessly in the world. Christ has gone "to prepare a place for us" in the heavenly realm of the Father.

The ascension of Christ won't let us forget the life that God offers us in Christ—eternal life—and we need to remember that "Gospel truth" in a world that emphasizes the personal, here-and-now gifts of the Gospel—courage to face life, support in facing problems, relief for a troubled conscience, hope in a hopeless world. So many of us forget God's final gift in favor of the immediate benefits of the Gospel and/or the church. We're like the native who lived next door to a Lutheran missionary in Africa—an old, blind hunter whose sight was restored when the missionary suspected that the blindness resulted from cataracts. Wesley Sadler, the missionary, arranged for examinations and, after positive diagnosis, an operation to remove the cataracts. After successful surgery and a period of recuperation, the old hunter returned home to his village where all of the people turned out to see what to them was a miracle. The next morning he was at Sadler's door early in the morning to thank him for his restored vision. And every day that the missionary was home the old man offered his gratitude for sight and a measure of new life. His daughter and her family were all baptized— but not the old hunter. He was thankful to God for what had been given him by His servants, but he never comprehended the greater gift being offered to him—eternal life. Whenever Sadler told the story, he added, "That's why the Gospel has to be preached to people in every part of the world." Eternal life, the Ascension reminds us, is ours.

Many of our congregations that light the Easter (Paschal) candle and burn it for the 40 days until the Ascension have adopted the practice of moving the Paschal candle to the baptismal font for the rest of the year. It is lighted again at every Baptism as a symbol of Christ's triumph over death in the Resurrection—and as a reminder that in the waters of the font we are given the gift of eternal life. When, in faith we relate the resurrection and ascension of the Lord to our lives, we become, as the disciples, "fools for Christ," laying down our lives and taking up our crosses and following Christ in loving service of God and people, and in the hope of life in the age to come. Amen.

Baptism—What We Have in Common

Ephesians 4:1-6

The true story of Eileen Steif and Chris Welna is a touching tale of love, devotion, and death in our times. Eileen and Chris met in college, became friends and fell in love only to learn that she had contracted cancer and would die. For the last three years of her life Chris was her devoted servant—caring for her, comforting her, even giving her "shots" to ease her pain. He gave up his own future—scholarships for study in Brazil and law school in the United States—because, he said, "She really needed a friend." When she finally died, he saw to it that her funeral was carried out as they had planned it. Only then when "it was all over" was he at all interested in considering himself and his future, his ambition, his vocation, his education, his life.

For the past three months or so we have considered another story of love, devotion, and death that reached a chilling climax on Good Friday and a twist on Easter Sunday. Jesus Christ died after a three-year ministry, His life of love and devotion to God and all people brought to an end by the very people He had come to save. But He arose "with a mighty victory o'er the grave" and a new and unending chapter in His life. And if Lent and Easter have really meant anything to us, perhaps we will comprehend that not only does Christ's "story" go on but we have an important part in it. The reality of the Resurrection drama—as God's "twist" in the "tale" of Jesus' love, devotion, and death—is just this: We can't simply go back and live out our lives as though nothing has really happened. If we have really kept the fast of Lent and celebrated the feast of Easter, our relationship with the Lord has to be deeper, our love for the Father has to be purer, and our commitment to the tasks He has given us to do in the world has to be more consuming.

The Sunday After the Ascension, as it used to be called, might only be the Seventh Sunday of Easter—or the last Sunday of Easter—but it is a good time to remember what has occurred during these 14 weeks since Ash Wednesday and attempt to fathom what it all means to and for us. The impact of that experience varies, of course, from person to person, and the results of it will bring forth different reactions and results in our lives, but there are certain benefits and blessings and obligations that we have in common. As Paul wrote to the Christians at Ephesus: "There is one body and one Spirit, just as you were called to the one hope that belongs to your call, one Lord, one faith, one baptism, one God and Father of us all, who is above all and through all and in all" (Eph. 4:4-6). In light of our Easter experience and this powerful statement by the apostle Paul, we ought to be convinced completely that we who have called Jesus "Lord" and God "Father" and have been baptized with water and the Spirit are indeed the children of God.

Christians Share Quality Living

To be a Christian is to live what might be called a "quality life." "Quality" in this case has to do with the relationships we have with God and each other, as well as our style and manner of life. The Christian's vocation is to live in love and harmony—in conscious and devoted relationship—with God and each other in our world. The Lent-Easter experience has taught us, once again, that we love God and one another "because He first loved us." God's love for us all in Jesus Christ makes this kind of a loving relationship possible; there's no way we can force ourselves to love God and all of His people apart from the love He imparts and implants in our hearts and souls.

The power of the Gospel story is simply incredible. Through that Word He is able to break down our defenses, invade our hearts and change them, no matter who we are, so that we become His loving children. Little children, perhaps especially and more easily than adults, appropriate the love of God. And even people of limited intelligence— the retarded—come to know the love that "passes knowledge" in Jesus Christ our Lord. A seminary student tells how he learned this valuable lesson while on a college choir tour in California. Between regularly scheduled concerts one day, the choir made an unscheduled stop and presented an impromptu concert at a home for retarded persons of all ages. Men and women, boys and girls, from the home were enchanted by the music of the college choir; they hardly moved during the concert. When it was over, through their supervisor they asked if they might sing for the choir. A teacher led them, and they sang simply—but with "glowing faces"—the first hymn that many of us learn as little children:

> Jesus loves me, this I know
> For the Bible tells me so.
> Little ones to Him belong;
> They are weak, but He is strong.
> Yes, Jesus loves me. Yes, Jesus loves me.
> Yes, Jesus loves me. The Bible tells me so.

126

Most of them couldn't read a word in the Bible, but they knew the story, and they knew that God loves them. To appropriate that love and to abide in it is the basis of living a life "worthy of our vocation" as Christians.

The "quality life" of the Christian includes a human dimension, too, because the relationship of love we abide in with God includes all other people as well. To limit our love to God, who alone is worthy of our love, is to love imperfectly. James Russell Lowell once wrote:

> That love for one from which there doth not spring
> Wide love for all is but a worthless thing.

At least, it is incomplete and one-sided—and, in the opinion of our Lord, impossible. Christ said, "He who does not love his brother whom he has seen cannot love God whom he has not seen" (1 John 4:20). He also declared, "A new commandment I give you, that you love one another; even as I have loved you" (John 13:34). And He also taught, "He who has My commandments, and keeps them, he it is who loves Me" (John 14:21). One-dimensional love is a complete contradiction of the Gospel simply because it belongs to a limited relationship—whether restricted to the human or to the divine.

Love for God cannot be measured in terms of worship and prayer or other acts of devotion, or even martyrdom, alone. The love we profess for God, which is part of our vocation, has to extend to His people through our acts of love and service to them. If we claim to love God, we have to use, in gratitude, whatever gifts He may have given us, not for our own glory, but for God's and for the benefit of other people. Whenever we pray, "Lord, I love You with all my heart and soul," we ought also to pray, "Let me use the gifts You have given me, including the new life and new relationship, with all my wisdom and strength for the blessing of others." That's the kind of quality of life that is "worthy of your vocation" as Christians.

Christians Share a "Bond of Peace"

The Christian's vocation is to love the members of the body of Christ and deal with them charitably, selflessly, gently, and patiently, according to the apostle. And that means always going the second, third, or even the fourth mile to preserve the work done by the Holy Spirit in establishing a "bond of peace" among us. The Christian is always suposed to "overcome evil" by returning "good for evil." That is a rather difficult thing to do, especially when other Christians offend us. But to do less than love and forgive others in the ways that Paul outlines is to break the "bonds of peace" God has established between us through the work of the Holy Spirit.

And the world we live in that is being ripped apart by hatred and violence desperately needs to see the "bond of peace" that is supposed to exist within the Christian community. A Christian physician and surgeon took his family on a tour of the mission fields of their denomination. They spent several of the winter months in Africa and visited most of Europe and, subsequently, they mailed a belated Christmas letter to friends and relatives, which arrived about the middle of Lent. The doctor made this observation: "The one thing that seemed to be most evident as we made our trip was the distrust and hatred of one group of people toward another, along with the poverty and needs in so many areas. What is the answer? It sounds very simple, I'm sure, but to me the answer is Christ in all of our hearts. Nothing else will make it possible to trust and love one another. God's gift of the Christ . . . is the answer." And you and I know, at the risk of oversimplifying the complex issues and answers of life, that he is right. We also know that those who do not belong to the Christian church need to observe deeds of love among the Christian communities and countries in addition to hearing the direct word of the Gospel. "They will know we are Christians by our love" for each other and for them. Too often they observe a lack of love among Christians and they miss, or refuse to accept, the whole point of preaching the Gospel in the world.

If we were all able to travel to modern Turkey and visit the ruins of Ephesus and the once-Christian churches in Istanbul and other parts of the country that once was so Christian, it would soon become apparent that we were in a Moslem, not a Christian, country. The Christians constitute a remnant of that once vital and vibrant mission field known as the "churches of Asia Minor." And we would most certainly wonder what went wrong. Why has the Christian faith been almost wiped out in the 20th century? The Christian Gospel was preached there for almost six centuries before the emergence of Mohammed the Prophet. Though the reasons for the decline of the Christian church are many and complicated in modern Turkey, we cannot but wonder what happened to the witness of those who live "in the bond of peace," not only in Turkey but in the rest of the world. Has Jesus Christ been rejected because of the failures of His body, His people? Did they see the Christians as a disruptive force, rather than a unifying element, in their society?

But Paul would weep, not only if he were able to visit Turkey and the ruins of that "marble city" built into the side of a hill but for us and our failure to "keep the unity of the Spirit in the bond of peace." And I suspect that our Lord might weep and would have wept many times in the past as He did over Jerusalem long ago: "Jerusalem, Jerusalem . . . ! How often would I have gathered your children together as a hen gathers her brood under her wings, and you would not!" (Luke 13:34). Could it be that we have been guilty of resisting the unifying power of the Holy Spirit? We sin against Father, Son, and Holy Spirit when we do not live up to our vocation—love for God and His people—and break the "bond of peace."

Christians Share "Oneness" in Christ

Perhaps it was his awareness of the divisions and divisiveness in the world and in the community of the believers over against "what ought to be," but Paul seems almost consumed with "oneness." He declares that there is "one body," "one Spirit," "one hope," "one Lord," "one faith," "one baptism," "one God and Father of us all." And he told the Galatians we share in that oneness "in Christ." He also informed them that as many as have been baptized into Christ have put on Christ. Baptism is the sacrament of our *oneness* in Christ and in his body, the church, here on earth. Baptism makes us His and "one in Him," whether we recognize and admit it, or not. That involves us in the business of being Christian and living out our lives in love for God and our fellow human beings.

It may have been because the Christians of the early church understood this so well that they made Pentecost a second baptismal festival. Some scholars believe that it was a sort of "reserve" date for those who were not ready to be baptized on Easter Sunday. But it would seem that Pentecost as the 50th day of Easter also became one of those special times when, remembering Easter and their baptism, Christians celebrated and prayed to God that "He would complete" what He had begun in Christ through the Holy Spirit.

This Sunday, between the Ascension and Pentecost, had to be— and should be for us—a time to recall what we have in common with each other in Christ and by our baptism. We are Christ's and we know that means we share all the blessings of God, including our hope in Christ, with each other, whether we are among the living or the dead. "Living or dying, we are the Lord's." Two professors of theology, one a Roman Catholic and a citizen of Rome, the other an American Lutheran, were discussing the life-styles and faith of Italian and American Christians. The professor-priest said, "If you really want to know what Italian Catholics believe, go out and visit our cemeteries." The Lutheran professor did just that and went to the Campo Verano, the only "active" cemetery in Rome. All Italian Christians from Rome are buried there. In the older part of the cemetery, which he entered first, the professor discovered that every grave seemed to have flowers (it was All Saints-All Souls time), many had photographs, all were above ground as if they were ready for the resurrection, and each grave had an "eternal light" burning before it. The new section was built as "high-rise mausoleums." Flowers, photographs, and fire were there, too. And the motif seemed to be that of the catacombs. Later, he went into an ancient church, the Church of St. Lawrence, where the remains of the third-century deacon-martyr lie beneath the main altar. Then he discovered that ancient catacombs extended out from that church like fingers reaching into the cemeteries—and the professor's message came into focus. Lawrence's church-grave is really the gravestone for the whole cemetery; he gave his life so that the poor of Rome might have bread to eat. He died because he refused to give the Roman emperor the "bread fund" of the church because he loved God's children as he loved God Himself. He could lay down his life for others because he believed that "God would lift him up" at the Last Day. All Christians who are buried there share that hope in common with Lawrence and each other. And we do, too!

And so today we take another "dip" into the font where we are washed clean, die and rise again, and realize that the new life we rise to in Christ our Lord is shared in common with all the children of God. Through His Spirit, He enables us to live as His loving children in the world. Amen.

Children of God

Romans 8:14-17, 22-27

Thomas D'Muhala, president of Nuclear Technologies Corporation of Amston, Conn., made an amazing statement to the newspapers after he and other scientists had made a trip to Italy to subject the Shroud of Turin to scientific tests of its authenticity. The shroud is the mysterious linen that supposedly was wrapped about the body of Christ and has an image of the crucified Christ imprinted on it. "We all thought we'd find it was a forgery and would be packing up our bags in a half hour," he said. "Instead, all of us who were there, at least all those I talked to, are convinced that the burden of proof has shifted. The burden is now on the skeptic."

Forty scientists were in the group that went to Italy on October 8, 1978, for six days of tests on the 3 x 14-foot shroud, which is locked in a silver casket and stored in a crypt behind the main altar of the Turin cathedral. D'Muhala declared that the "three-dimensional image on the cloth is that of Jesus and was 'projected' on the surface, perhaps by a burst of some kind of radiation emanating from all parts of the body in a two-thousandths-of-a-second flash." The scientists "determined the man on the cloth had been crucified, suffered a very deep and bloody wound on his side, endured 120 lashes and numerous deep wounds around the head." D'Muhala noted that "those wounds would correspond to the Biblical account of the torture endured by Christ." And he added, "Every one of the scientists I have talked to believe the cloth is authentic. . . . Some say maybe this is a love letter, a tool He left behind for the analytical mind."

Such speculation, scientific or otherwise, is interesting; but it is not determinative for the existence, or quality, of our faith. The Holy Spirit bears witness to the reality of our relationship with God in Jesus Christ the Lord. Through water and the Spirit God puts His mark on us and seals us into His kingdom. The Spirit brings the work of Christ to us and gives us the faith we need to receive it. He restores us to that relationship that was ours in the beginning as children of God. Pentecost celebrates the coming of God's promised power that breaks down the walls that separate us from each other and from our Creator. It is the festival of restoration, wherein we know with certainty that God is our Father and we are His children, as Paul perceives, "All who are led by the Spirit of God are sons of God. . . . When we cry, 'Abba! Father!' it is the Spirit Himself bearing witness with our spirit that we are children of God" (Rom. 8:14-16). Spirit-given and Spirit-filled faith tells us that we are God's children for time and eternity.

Pentecost is the festival of the new creation. The Word and the Spirit are set free in the world once more to renew and restore God's creatures. We were washed clean in the River, and emerge from the waters of Baptism to hear a heavenly voice saying, "You are My beloved children." The Holy Spirit assures us we are and will be God's children in life and in death, and that God has been telling us this in our baptism and ever since.

The Spirit Teaches Us to Say, "Father"

In response to the assurance in Baptism that we are God's children, the Spirit teaches us to answer His word of blessing with "Father." With this the relationship between God and ourselves is complete; we know He loves us—the cross of Christ tells us that as nothing else could. The death of Christ is always an expression of the depth of the Father's love for His children; this was the only way that God could forgive us our sins and grant us new life through reconciliation with Himself while retaining His integrity as our God. The Father shared in Jesus' pain and passion; and His healing love played an active role in the Son's obedient, but bloody, sacrifice. To word it differently: "In Christ God was reconciling the world to Himself" (2 Cor. 5:19). The Spirit enlightens us as we look at the cross, so that we might understand that our Father was responsible for what happened at Calvary.

And so the Holy Spirit helps us to understand the sufferings and death of Christ on our behalf—that it was "to give us life"—that is, make us God's children again—that He suffered and bled and died. A St. Paul, Minn., newspaper carried an unusual story last Christmas about a 22-year-old mother—divorced and trying to feed, clothe, and house her three children, on about $450 from welfare. She had no money for Christmas presents, so she did the only thing she could think of; she went to a blood bank and sold six pints of her blood at $5.00 per pint over a three-week period. When she returned for the seventh time, she was sent home because she was too weak to give any more blood. She told a reporter, "This is the roughest Christmas I have ever had." When the children learn and come to appreciate what she did for them that Christmas, and how much she loved them, they will remember it as the

132

"best" Christmas they have ever had. The story of her sacrifice reminds us of another, a sacrifice for all people, so that everyone in the world who looks at it as his own can call God "Father" again.

Henceforth, we know that nothing we may do "will separate us from the love of God in Christ Jesus our Lord." Listen to the way that Paul sums up all of this to the church at Rome: "If God is for us, who is against us? He did not spare His own Son but gave Him up for us all, will He not also give us all things with Him? . . . Who shall separate us from the love of Christ? . . . For I am sure that neither death, nor life, nor angels, nor principalities, nor things present, nor things to come, nor powers, nor height, nor depth, nor anything else in all creation will be able to separate us from the love of God in Christ Jesus our Lord" (Rom. 8:31-32, 35, 38-39). The Spirit convinces us that through the cross of Christ the Father floods the world with His love so as to wash away any doubts we may have about Him and His concern for us.

The Spirit Teaches Us to Hope

Someone has said that it is getting more and more difficult to live and have any hope for the future. The world is impersonal and cruel; people care about themselves first of all, about others if they have anything left over. Not a few people contend that it has to be this way; the economy threatens financial well-being, political unrest in the world is a menace to peace, and the "bomb" almost makes irrelevant the concerns we have about the environment, overpopulation, depletion of natural resources, the energy crisis, and the masses of poverty-stricken people here upon the earth crying out for justice and a bit of bread. The future sometimes looks hopeless in spite of our echoing Paul's, "I am sure that . . . [nothing] will be able to separate us from the love of God in Christ Jesus our Lord" (Rom. 8:38-39).

But the Holy Spirit helps us to believe that God really does have "the whole world in His hands," that He *is* in charge and His will is going to be done in the end. We are able to state with Paul that "in everything God works for good with those who love Him, who are called according to His purpose" (Rom. 8:28). There is no such thing as hopelessness or a hopeless world for the Christian; a Christian lives in hope and by hope, despite the apparent hopelessness of the human situation in the world. Only we Christians may dare to believe that God turns all things to our good when we love and trust Him. That's informed hope, not blind and oversimplified optimism. We entrust our lives to Him in faith and hope. Our Father loves us and can be trusted!

Even in the face of death we may trust Him, recognizing with the apostle that "we wait for . . . the redemption of our bodies. For in this hope we were saved. We hope for what we do not see" (Rom. 8:23-25).

Lent was approaching its climax one year when James Anderson spoke in a chapel service. He spoke, he said, "some words . . . which have been hammered out on the anvil of my own personal agony, tears and struggle of the last two weeks." He told the story of Pammy Emberson, a member of his congregation and a senior in one of the local high schools. He said she was a lovely young lady with a pleasing personality, intelligence, and ambition; she seemed to have a great future. But Pammy began to have headaches and double vision, which led to surgery twice during the fall of her senior year to relieve pressure on her brain. A brain tumor was discovered in January. She received cobalt treatments and was unable to attend school. She studied with a homebound teacher in the hope that she would soon recover and be able to return to school in time to be graduated with her class. But in the middle of Lent she was hospitalized once more; she asked her doctors to "put it on the line" and learned that she had only days to live. On Friday of that week she requested Holy Communion, with her family and pastor. The next Tuesday a group of her friends visited her and a moving service of song, praise, and healing took place. Pastor Anderson said, "She confronted each person with a joyous and triumphant Christianity" and teenagers who had given God just a passing nod before came out of her room shaken and moved to the depths of their souls by her witness. There was in her vibrant testimony something of that quality that Cardinal Suhard once defined: "To be a witness does not consist in engaging in propaganda, nor even in stirring people up, but in being a living mystery. It means to live in such a way that one's life would make no sense if God did not exist." Her friends could not comprehend how she could face death without fear and with a joyous hope.

At the end of that week, 30 of her classmates, her pastor, the principal of her high school, and the chairperson of the school board crowded into her room, draped a graduation gown over her shoulders, and presented her with a diploma. Pam's father took pictures: "Then she asked everybody to leave for a minute except me [her pastor]. She looked up at me and said, 'I am happy. . . . I know we are going to meet again.' I answered, 'It will be a far better place than this.' She looked up at me and said, 'See you there.' That night she died in her sleep saying words that her mother heard like 'graduation,' 'Jefferson,' 'finals,' 'Jesus.'"

"What more is there to say," asked the pastor, "but that in the confusion, in the mystery of our lives, the cross has become the hand of God extended for us to hold. . . . But life must go on somehow. . . . On Easter Sunday everything will be all right. Everything will be good." The Spirit convinces us of that, and so, no matter what happens in life or death, we abide in the hope of Bunyan's pilgrim for whom "all the trumpets sounded on the other side."

The Spirit Teaches Us to Live

Because we know that God is our Father and invites us to call Him "Father" and trust and hope in Him, the fear of the unknown—death and ultimate destruction—is banished from our lives. This means that we are free of fear and therefore free to "throw away our lives" by "being fools for Christ." While most people in this world think of themselves, their desires, wants, and ambitions, we, under the Spirit's insistent teaching, recognize our responsibility to God and our fellow human beings as determinative for the way we live in the world. As children of God, restored by the Cross and Baptism, we have the basic love of Christ in our hearts. We are changing the way we do things, the way we think about our needs, and the way we set our priorities, simply because love compels us to.

But we desperately need to realize that our baptism means that through us God has given the whole world another chance. We have been made new creatures, and the whole world is in our hands. We have the Gospel to share, and we are to be at this God-given task until "Christ comes again."

The Star Thrower, the title of one of four posthumously published books by Loren Eiséley, is also the title of a chapter in *The Unexpected Universe*. Eiseley has gone to Costabel, whose "beaches are littered with the debris of life." People go there to collect shells washed up by the tide and tremendous storms. Shortly after he arrived there, a violent storm awakened him; an insomniac, he could not get back to sleep. He saw the lights of the "professional pickers," as he called them, on the beach before dawn. He went down to observe what they were doing. As he watched the "pickers" and saw various forms of sea life thrown up on the beach by storm and tide, he became conscious of the wind and made for a point along the steep shore that might offer "refuge" from it. The sun was just rising, and he writes: "Ahead of me, over the projecting point, a gigantic rainbow of incredible perfection had sprung shimmering into existence. Somewhere toward its foot I discerned a human figure standing, it seemed to me, within the rainbow . . . gazing fixedly at something in the sand." Eiseley walked toward the man—and the rainbow receded.

When Loren Eiseley approached the man he discovered that the man was looking at a starfish that "had thrust its arms up stiffly and was holding its body away from the stifling mud." Eiseley said, "It's still alive." The stranger replied, "Yes," and "With a quick yet gentle movement," Eiseley said, "he picked up the star and spun it over my head and far out into the sea." "It may live," the man said, "if the offshore pull is strong enough." Eiseley said to him, "There are not many who come this far. . . . Do you collect?" "Only like this," the star thrower answered, "and only for the living. . . . The stars throw well. One can help them." Eiseley says, "He looked at me with a faint question in his eyes . . . ," and replied, "I do not collect. . . . Neither the living nor the dead. I gave it up long ago. Death is the only successful collector." He nodded good-bye, retraced his steps, and as he rounded a bend and looked back, Eiseley "saw him toss another star. . . . For a moment, in the changing light, the thrower appeared magnified, as though casting larger stars upon some greater sea. He had, at any rate, the posture of a god."

Eiseley states that from his perspective "the star thrower was mad, and his particular acts were a folly from which I had chosen not to associate myself. I was an observer and a scientist. Nevertheless, I had seen the rainbow attempting to attach itself to the earth." Unable to sleep or get the star thrower out of his mind, and after another storm, he set out to find the man again. He found him with a rainbow at dawn, on the wind-swept beach as before: "Silently I sought and picked up a still-living star, spinning it far out into the waves. I spoke once briefly. 'I understand. . . . Call me another thrower.'" And he adds, "Only then I allowed myself to think. He is not alone any longer. After us there will be others."

At the end of the story, Loren Eiseley remarks: "I picked up a star whose tube feet ventured timidly among my fingers while, like a true star, it cried soundlessly for life. I saw it with an unaccustomed clarity and cast far out. With it, I flung myself . . . into some unknown dimension of existence. . . ."

Our experience of the Word in the water and the Spirit is something like that—only the Man we have seen was nailed to a cross. The rainbow—God's promise—is connected to the earth through that Man. And the Spirit convinces us that it was for us that He threw—not a starfish—but His life away. And knowing that we are children of God, too, we may boldly follow Him and throw our lives away in the knowledge that God will forever take care of His own. And so we pray:

Father in heaven, at the Baptism of Jesus in the River Jordan You proclaimed Him your beloved Son and anointed Him with the Holy Spirit. Make all who are baptized into Christ faithful in their calling to be Your children and inheritors with Him of everlasting life; through Your Son, Jesus Christ, our Lord, who lives and reigns with You and the Holy Spirit, one God, now and forever. Amen.